STONE circles

This book is dedicated to John Martineau

Acknowledgements

Grateful thanks are due to the following people for help, advice and free access to information and materials: Rodney Castleden, David Furlong, Helen Green at Hodder Headline, John Martineau, John Michell, Hamish Miller, Teresa Moorey, Mike Powells and Dave Davidge at the Alexander Keiller Museum, Avebury, the late Dr Archie Thom and the many other friends, students and circle enthusiasts who promote interest in the ancient ways.

Figures 3.6b, 4.2, 4.5a, 4.5b, 4.7a, 4.7b and 4.8 were first published in *Megalithic Sites in Britain* by Alexander Thom (Oxford University Press, 1967) © Oxford University Press. The author and publishers would like to thank Oxford University Press for their permission to reproduce them.

Order queries: please contact Bookpoint Ltd, 39 Milton Park, Abingdon, Oxon OX14 4TD. Telephone: (44) 01235 400414, Fax: (44) 01235 400454. Lines are open from 9.00–6.00, Monday to Saturday, with a 24-hour message answering service. Email address: orders@bookpoint.co.uk

British Library Cataloguing in Publication Data
A catalogue record for this title is available from The British Library

ISBN 0 340 73772 7

First published 1999
Impression number   10 9 8 7 6 5 4 3 2 1
Year   2005 2004 2003 2002 2001 2000 1999

Copyright © 1999 Robin Heath

Typeset by Transet Limited, Coventry, England.
Printed in Great Britain for Hodder & Stoughton Educational, a division of Hodder Headline plc, 338 Euston Road, London NW1 3BH by Cox and Wyman Limited, Reading, Berks.

CONTENTS

Introduction   1

Chapter 1   Before the beginning — A brief history of British Culture from 3500 bce   5

Pushing back the dates   6
The days of the Celts and Romans   7
Christianity and the new cult of the cross   8
The death of the 'devilish' stones   10
Summary   12

Chapter 2   Stone Circles — Location and Purpose   13

Sticks and stones – how to preserve culture for 5,000 years   16
Cultural continuity and sacred geometry   17
The place of the dead   19
The gathering of the tribe   21
The astronomic connection   24
The geometry of stone circles   25
Summary   26

Chapter 3   The patterns of the past – a Geomancy Primer I   27

Archaeologists behaving badly   29
A realistic technology   30
The leyline problem   31
Alignments – making straight lines   33
Megalithic stone rows   38
Triangles   42
Circles   44
The year, the month and the day drawn out   48
Summary   48

Chapter 4   Stone circles which are not circular – a Geomancy Primer II   49

Ellipses   49
Flattened circles   53
Stone egg-shaped rings   56
Compound rings   61
Concentric rings   62
Summary   65

Chapter 5   Who Visits Stone Circles?   67

Archaeology   67
Archaeo-astronomy   68
Metrology, sacred geometry and geomancy   69
Leyhunting and dowsing   71
The shamanistic approach   73

Chapter 6   Understanding Megalithic Astronomy   75

The dance of the Sun and Moon   76
The breath of the Moon   79
The numbers of the Sun and Moon   80
Eclipses   83

The stars   85
The planets   86
Summary   87

Chapter 7   The Re-emergence of Megalithic Science   88

The megalithic legacy as calendraic artefacts   88
The numbers of the evolutionary engine   89
The irrational calendar   90
Thirteen months *versus* twelve months   91
The megalithic legacy as folklore and legend (solar heroes
    and sleeping beauties)   91
Sexing the stones   92
The silver fraction   93
The lunation triangle   95
Biblical and geomantic messages from the past   97
Summary   99

Appendix: The top twenty UK sites to visit   100

Further Reading   105

INTRODUCTION

Mysterious, brooding and enigmatic, stone circles are the enduring remains of an ancient culture which predated the Celts, the Romans, the Anglo-Saxons, the Normans and, more recently, the European Union. Whilst the majority of the remains of this culture have all but vanished from the landscape, it is possible to glimpse traces of a megalithic science from these stone rings, constructions which have endured the ravages of much time and many human cultural changes.

Stone circles invite speculation as to their origins – older than history, they are the skeletons of a prehistoric belief system, terribly remote from us and therefore enchanting. In writing this guide I have suggested a wide variety of practical exercises which will place the reader in the same mindset as the megalithic architects employed, these tasks involving the identical techniques which led to most of the known shapes of stone rings and their associated astronomy. I have made the assumption that *doing* is, wherever possible, preferable to merely reading or *thinking* about a subject. That said, this book will also leave you with a great deal to think about!

It was said by a great contemporary mythologist, the late Joseph Campbell, that if one wishes to know the priorities of a culture – what a culture worships – one has only to look at the nature and purpose of the most imposing buildings that culture erects. Today it is Canary Wharf, not so long ago (only 600 years or so!) it was the great cathedrals and, if we go back over 5,000 years, stone circles and allied megalithic monuments. Between 3,000 and 5,000 years ago the most imposing, enduring and commonly erected stone structures in Europe, particularly along the western seaboard of the

North Atlantic, were stone rings – thousands of them! So what is known about these strange constructions?

- Some stone circles have a geometry which is astonishingly complex.
- The local astronomy of the site, particularly the rising and setting cycles of the Sun and Moon, is often incorporated into the design.
- These structures were incorporated with the treatment of the dead.
- The builders everywhere were using the same units of length.

This is enough information to apply Joseph Campbell's criterium and thus define the cultural priorities of the megalith builders, i.e. we need to concentrate on the geometry, astronomy, technology and ritual purposes of stone circles.

For over 2,000 years, perhaps five of these monuments were erected each year, each one involving a huge expenditure of man-hours, which included the removal, carriage and accurate placement of huge stones, often from sources miles away from the location. These designs aroused a strong motivation in the community – they were labours of devotional love, taking thousands of hours to complete. The geometric designs for these rings may still be read from the survivors, and these inform us of how consistently certain patterns were repeated throughout the whole region for maybe two millennia. Their incorporation of local astronomic phenomena into the design is another consistent feature of these designs. We will consider how this can be, when there were apparently no plans, no Department of Industry and no building regulations in neolithic Britain. How did a preliterate, primitive culture produce and maintain such marvels of technique, astronomy and geometry?

We can already glimpse why we find it so hard to understand this culture. Our present culture regards geometry as profoundly boring – most school-leavers thinking it holds no relevance to our times. No other culture of educated people has ever held such a viewpoint. The treatment of the dead remains a taboo in our present culture – a subject riddled with euphemisms, jokes and fear. The widespread ignorance of basic astronomy, particularly the motions of the Moon and Sun represents another huge departure from previous cultures. The culture which erected the circles was apparently nearly

obsessed with such things and I have attempted to provide answers as to why in this text.

RECONNECTING TO THE SACRED

Today we live in a culture which has progressively dumped the sacred and thinks, erroneously, that science and the sacred cannot be happy bedfellows. Within the scale of human evolution, this is a remarkably recent, some would say arrogant, departure from what has always been before. In truth our modern world runs on rails laid down on a ballast of sacred geometry and the observation of planetary phenomena – from great and devout men like Johannes Kepler, who used ancient sacred geometry to discover his planetary laws, the only planetary laws of any import discovered to this day; and Newton, who aspired through alchemy, sacred geometry and mathematics, to understand the laws of nature via the legacy of past civilizations. Through his observations of the Moon he discovered the law of gravity, which led to the universal laws of motion. The twentieth century could not have happened without either of these gentlemen, whose source material – observations of the solar system – formed one of the main pre-occupations of the circle builders.

If our present culture has since failed utterly to integrate the sacred within its apparently rational world view, then it is clear that our circle builders were totally committed to working with sacred space, the circles of the sky, the Sun and the Moon, long before any Roman charioted his way to Britain. Neolithic and Bronze Age culture began discovering the mathematics and geometry of nature's patterns long before the main flowering of Egyptian or Greek culture. Their 'proofs' still lie neglected on practically every hill and moor in Europe, huge monuments consisting of stone circles, standing stones and henges. And we ignore them, perhaps because our history books do, perhaps because they frighten us a little, and almost certainly because we arrogantly assume that they have nothing to tell us about life on Earth. Stone circles *are* mysterious and not at all well understood by our culture, and we shall look at the reasons for this.

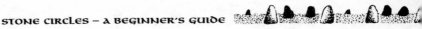

In the 1960s, a few people wrote 'groovy' books which recovered some of the information about this subject from our ancestral past. Bligh Bond, Keith Critchlow, John Michell and Alexander Thom were just some of the pioneers of this modern revival in sacred geometry, sacred sites and sacred space. In that monumental decade, alongside the sex, drugs and rock 'n' roll, folk everywhere looked for renewed meaning in their lives, and in the relationships and rituals they hold with the Earth, Mother Nature and the Cosmos. Stone circles demonstrated to this new generation that all these things had been an important part of neolithic European life a long, long time ago.

This book is ultimately about how you can discover more meaning in your life through practical approaches to the sacred spaces of the megalithic culture. You will learn a lot, have some fun and connect to something which has permeated human life for thousands of years, long before the 'blip' which produced our present materialist industrial culture obscured it. What will you learn? Undoubtedly, that visiting and studying these ancient sites connects us with our ancestors. Astonishingly, when it comes to understanding the planet we have inherited from them, they still have a great deal to tell us. We can, therefore, learn humility from our forebears – the circle builders understood basic astronomy better than any medieval astronomer, and most educated moderns will, alas, have to face their almost total ignorance in these matters, and in simple geometry, when they meet the megalithic culture. The stone circles are the cultural bones of our ancestors and, after 5,000 years, they still have something vital to say to us.

BEFORE THE BEGINNING

A Brief History of British Culture from 3500 BCE

The biggest single problem we face in trying to place ourselves within the mindset of megalithic people is not a lack of physical evidence concerning their culture, for substantial stone remains still litter the wilder places around the British Isles, their skeletons and burial finery abound in reasonable numbers and the remains of their round houses, even their dressers, cooking arrangements and domestic rubbish may be picked over and studied. The problem we face is that megalithic folk apparently did not write down anything of what they were up to. They were *pre-literate*. Consequently, those Egyptian hieroglyphics and the thousands of Babylonian cuneiform clay tablets sent historians scurrying towards the Middle East in their search for the roots of culture.

It is certainly true that a culture whose history can be read off walls, papyrus and clay tablets tends to get studied and understood better than one which cannot. The megalithic culture appeared to our Victorian and Edwardian ancestors as dull, primitive and frankly rather boring when placed alongside the splendour that was then being pulled out of tombs in Egypt. A further factor made the 'stones and bones' of Britain even less interesting to the public – the experts of the time erroneously reckoned they were much more recent than the artefacts from the Middle Eastern cultures – some even thought they were Roman.

Pushing Back the Dates

Since the Second World War, the dating of stone circles, tumuli and burial chambers has been steadily pushed back so that it is more or less true that one must add between 500 and 1,500 years to the dating suggested in books written during the 1950s and early 1960s. Stonehenge's earliest constructions now pan out at 3100 BCE, whereas it is still possible in the brochures and books on sale at the monument to find 1750 BCE as the 'official' date. The revised dating places Stonehenge half a millennium *before* the building of the Great Pyramid and thus Britain's megalithic culture *predates* many of the main achievements of the famous Middle Eastern cultures of antiquity. This requires an enormous change of historical perspective, one which has only just begun to percolate through into the history books.

The history of the megalithic culture was never chronicled properly and, for various reasons, it would have been impossible to write an accurate historical account after the era of stone circle building finished. After 1450 BCE, circle building rapidly became unimportant to the society. Perhaps we should now ask why?

One theory is that climatic catastrophe took the weather in Britain from that of a present-day Spain to the damp and cloudy climate Britain 'enjoys' today. Volcanic dust emissions are blamed for making the northern parts of Britain uninhabitable within a single generation, and a mass exodus of people is evidenced. Astronomical observations would also have become impossibly difficult, due to cloud, and neither would the huge numbers of man-hours have been available to build these stone observatories and temples if the people were truly struggling to provide their basic needs. The culture which built the circles clearly had time on its hands.

Other theories include cosmic catastrophy. A large asteroid is thought by some academics to have hit the Earth sometime in the third millennium BCE, causing widespread havoc, a 'nuclear winter' and corresponding huge social and cultural changes. Final proof remains to be found. Whatever did occur, it remains true that the era of building stone circles passed out of fashion with extreme suddenness after 1450 BCE. For over two millennia prior to that date,

perhaps five large stone circles were erected each year in the British Isles, Ireland and Brittany. After 1450 BCE, perhaps only a dozen examples have been dated, most of these doubtfully, and *none* are known after 1000 BCE. Circle building finished extremely quickly once it had had its day.

The days of the Celts and Romans

The Celts occupied the British Isles from about 1250 BCE onwards and presumably inherited some knowledge concerning the stone circle builder's art and intentions. Valuable evidence of Celtic expertise in astronomy has been discovered recently and it is clear that revision of this culture must include a deeper respect for its fascination with sacred geometry. The five-year soli-lunar *Coligny Calendar*, which dates from about the fifth century BCE, is an example of Celtic wisdom in the calendraic arts.

Seven centuries after the Celts arrived, the expanding Roman Empire steadily made invasive inroads into Britain, their soldiers reporting in letters to their families of a highly sophisticated and ordered society, whilst Caesar wrote *officially* of 'woad-covered savages'. The political advantages of his stance are time honoured and, in this case, allowed the Romans to take credit for having built all those wonderful straight roads that criss-cross the British Isles – many of which were already in place before they arrived and were merely modified to take heavier chariots.

Successful invaders *always* rewrite the history of the culture they have vanquished and belittle its achievements. In this political climate it would, therefore, have been most unlikely and unwise for any historian, Roman or otherwise, to have written glowingly of any Celtic practice, including advanced astronomical and calendrical techniques. Even so, we do have some written evidence of high culture. The single garment most valued by Romans in fashion-conscious Rome was the *Sagi*, a Celtic cloak, woven in Britain. Such savages, Britons were!

The Romans introduced their revised 365-day calendar in 45 BCE, whence any other forms of time-keeping were made illegal throughout the Empire. Following this date, it would also have been most unwise to have pointed out that the original Brits had once enjoyed a much better calendar system which facilitated the prediction of eclipses. Again, the cultural pressure was to malign or ignore what had been going on here in order to pave the way for the Brave New Roman Empire.

CHRISTIANITY AND THE NEW CULT OF THE CROSS

Christianity arrived in Britain soon after the alleged date of the crucifixion. The Romans never actually conquered Ireland nor parts of Wales and it was in these regions that the Celtic saints, who originally brought the messages of the early Christian Church to the western parts of Britain, were actively promoting the original Christian philosophy safe from Roman persecution. This faith was different from the later doctrines of the Roman Church and, interestingly, there appears to have been little conflict between the tenets of Celtic Paganism and those of Celtic Christianity.

After 360 CE, the Roman Empire began to disintegrate, leaving the Celts fighting for their cultural life against the inroads in eastern Britain from the Anglo-Saxon barbarians. The Celtic monks, David, Illtud, Sampson, Gildas, Patrick and a host of lesser pious men and women, held access to the records and secrets of the Celtic culture. St Illtud set up a monastic school at *Llanilltud Fawr* (now Llantwit Major) in South Wales, to which the sons and daughters of rich Europeans were sent in order to be educated into the cultural legacy of Celtic and Christian life.

It is interesting to consider how it was possible that the pagan Celts adopted Christianity throughout their kingdom without any major cultural protest. Might it be that the original Christianity owed much of its background to cultural influences from Irish and Celtic thought?

For example, even as late as the tenth century, long after the invasion by the Anglo-Saxon barbarians was over, the monasteries of Celtic Britain contained poetry and verse which clearly revealed the hidden and suppressed past of the megalith builders. Celtic society preserved its many secrets through song, legend and verse – the *bardic tradition*. The astronomical texts in *Saltair na Rann* (see page 15) were not opposed to original Christian thought, unlike the Roman Church's later approach to astronomical truths and pagan practices.

When the Christianity of Rome arrived in force into Britain, circa 600 CE, its proponents found a country where the megalithic sites were still important to the ceremonies and spiritual beliefs of the majority of Celts and their newly civilized conquerors, the Anglo-Saxons. To convert the population to Christianity – at least the Roman Church's version of it – required that certain time-honoured tactics, brainwashing and fear, be liberally applied. They were.

The history of the Church's attacks on Paganism – 'The Old Religion', certainly included megalithic monuments, and the effects of countless generations worth of honest people being told not to become involved in the 'devilish' stones, evil circles, tumuli, etc, can only be guessed, although the map of Britain on page 14 shows this to have been a nationwide phenomenon. One has only to glance at the names of many of Britain's most famous megalithic sites to see the link being forged between ancient sites and their connection with evil and disobedience of God's law. The Devil's Quoit and the Devil Stones are two rather obvious examples, as is the vast folklore concerning revellers whose antics at these sites, on the Sabbath day and often connected with dancing, music or sexual freedom, caused the good Lord to turn them into stones. Examples of this genre include the Merry Maidens, the Piper's Stones and the Hurlers. Other names conjure up giants, witches, dragons and monsters. No wonder the majority of the population became nervous of such places, building up over many generations a fear of any relic of the megalithic culture. This fear still lurks deep in the national psyche.

Pope Gregory the Great (590–604 CE) described the British as a nation, 'placed in an obscure corner of the world, … hitherto … wholly taken up with the adoration of wood and stones'. He then

dispatched St Augustine from Rome and England in 596 CE to attempt to change this state of affairs. A century later, at least on paper, the process appeared complete and successful, yet edicts issued by the Church until at least 1100 CE tell the observant historian a somewhat different story. Augustine's instructions, direct from Rome, were to destroy the pagan idols *by building Christian churches on the same sites*. In all parts of the British Isles today, the casual observer will find churches built on mounds, tumps, ancient crossroads and even stone circles. In Brittany, to comply with the Pope's dictates, some churches had to incorporate immoveable megaliths within their superstructure! In truth, these apparently cunning tactics to eradicate pagan sites ensured exactly the opposite, and many of them were thereby preserved in a Christian aspic and thus spared the plough and the ravages of subsequent progress. Churchyards still remain one of the best hunting grounds for megalithic remains.

The death of the 'devilish' stones

In the *Laws of Knut* it is stated that, even after 1000 CE, the main objects of worship in England were 'The Sun and Moon, fire and water, springs, stones and trees'. King Knut banned all of this, of course, but this was as effective as trying to stop incoming tides, another of King Knut's famous failures. By the fourteenth century, the huge Avebury stones in Wiltshire were being systematically attacked and many of its finest stones were steam-split and carted away. People died during these vandalous acts; a barber who was crushed to death by a stone was left where he fell, under the stone. His scissors were found with his skeleton and are now in the Alexander Keiller Museum at Avebury.

A persistent legend informs us that the demolition of a megalithic site will invoke a curse on the destroyers, their families and the land surrounding the site. Even so, this was not enough to prevent John 'Stonekiller' Robinson becoming a local hero for supplying Avebury villagers with 'building stone'. He was taken to task in the village

church by no less than the brilliant antiquary, William Stukeley himself, in 1724, for his misdeeds. But no evident curse befell him other than his name is now immortalized, in stone one might say, as the prime desecrator of the world's largest stone circle.

With the invention of dynamite and hard-tipped drills in the nineteenth century, many sites were blasted out of the fields they had stood in for 4,000 years, their stumps – with 2.5 cm (1 inch) diameter drill holes still visible to the observant – a tragic testimony to this ill-judged action. Attempts to remove megalithic sites still continue to this day. Even in the supposedly enlightened twentieth century, sites have been ploughed up, stones removed, burial chambers filled in and a host of more minor desecrations have been perpetrated. Many otherwise educated folk, who care passionately about 'heritage', remain surprisingly indifferent to this destruction; perhaps they would do well to remember Alex Thom's remark,

> *The clues which eventually led ... to the unravelling of the geometry of Avebury did not come from Stonehenge or Stanton Drew but from small unimpressive circles on the Scottish moors and the hills of Wales.*

And whilst one might think that Stonehenge, in Wiltshire, which appears to have escaped the worst attentions of the earlier anti-pagans, might now rest in peace, we discover, unbelievably, that a demand was made by the military authorities in 1917 to completely demolish Stonehenge as '... its stones constituted a dangerous hazard to low-flying aircraft.'

The single biggest problem to those who wish to destroy megalithic sites is that removal of the stones still leaves a whopping stone hole, and any archaeologist will tell you that it is impossible to remove a hole; even filling it in won't remove the evidence! From this evidence the original geometry of a ruined site can often be recovered, as we shall explore later in this book. Despite the antics of the human race and all that the British weather has thrown at them over the past 5,000 years, Stonehenge, Avebury and a large number of other sites *have* survived, and it is from these artefacts that we must piece together the reasons why such things once occupied our ancestors for over 2,000 years. What were the criteria for building a megalith?

Similarly, folk culture and legends cannot be destroyed. Just as it was impossible to destroy Avebury, other patterns of the cultural past remain resolutely in place deep in the nation's psyche and within its folklore, even if often hidden from conscious expression. The many legends surrounding the megaliths, passed down through many generations, can also inform us about their purpose. This is another valid way of piecing together clues about our past, because the legends can be placed alongside the objective information from archaeologists, anthropologists, astronomers and geometers.

Summary

From this brief account of Britain's rich and colourful history we can see much more clearly why knowledge of the activities of the megalith builders disappeared or went underground. Until the twentieth century, Britain remained politically 'Roman' and the sanctioned Christianity was basic Catholicism diluted with two parts of water. Thus, the 'Old Religion' remained dangerous stuff well into the twentieth century, to be discouraged wherever it was found, and stone circles and standing stones remained 'the work of the Devil'. Before then, in a culture where most people received no formal education and where few could read, it was easy to promote and maintain the state of ignorance and fear concerning the megaliths. Even so, there is a multitude of evidence to suggest that the Templars, Cathars, Freemasons, Rosicrucians and certain Druidic and monastic orders well understood and carried forward the legacy of this past culture, even though guarding their secrets zealously within hermetic orders.

The twentieth-century State has found different demons with which to occupy itself, and the Church's power has become so weakened that it is safe once again to study this aspect of our past without too much fear of persecution. The conditions have become ripe for people once again to look the old megalithic 'devil' right in the face. Or, as a remarkable retired Scottish professor of engineering did, by 'keeking' down the eye piece of a theodolite (see Chapter 3).

STONE CIRCLES – LOCATION AND PURPOSE

In this chapter we attempt to find out what a stone circle may have represented to its builders and what it can reveal to modern-day visitors. We shall discover that there are several general and useful truths underpinning these fascinating artefacts from our ancient past.

Most megalithic artefacts, including stone circles, are to be found on the western side of the British Isles, as the map (Figure 2.1) indicates. The exception is eastern Scotland, although in eastern Ireland, specifically the Wicklow Mountains, there are also some fine examples. These areas also coincide with a geological structure which comprises mainly igneous (volcanic basalt) rocks and a more mountainous terrain. The stones used for stone circles are usually igneous or very hard sedimentary rocks – the circles were intended to last! The eastern side of England is rather deficient in suitable stone and, in addition, the flatter countryside encouraged clearance and ploughing which, over the centuries, has destroyed many megalithic sites.

Paul Devereux, in his interesting book, *Earthlights*, shows how the distribution of megalithic monuments tallies very closely indeed with the geology of Britain, particularly emphasizing a link between geological fault lines and stone circles. He suggests that the occurrence of balls of light around ancient sacred sites and along 'leylines' is a feature more connected to the geology of faulting and associated plasma production than to any supernatural causes or UFOs. [*Earthlights* by Paul Devereux, published (1982) by Turnstone Press. ISBN 085500 123 2.]

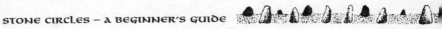

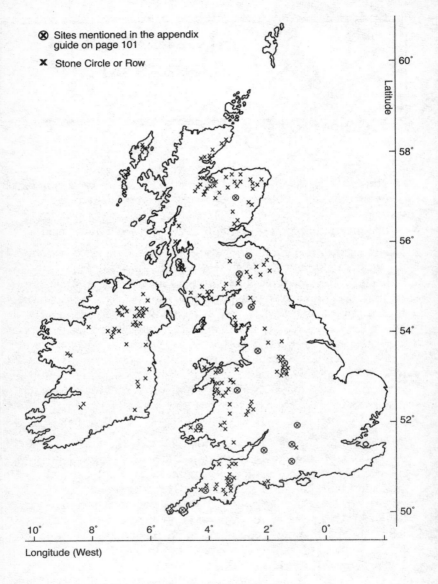

⊗ Sites mentioned in the appendix
guide on page 101

✖ Stone Circle or Row

Latitude

60°

58°

56°

54°

52°

50°

10°   8°   6°   4°   2°   0°

Longitude (West)

Figure 2.1 Megalithic circles in the United Kingdom

14

However, there are other interesting theories as to why circles and standing stones predominate on the western side of north-western Europe. It is here where the highest tides in the world may be found, and tides are connected with the Moon. The tides around the British Isles indicate that the power of the Moon is greatest here. Almost certainly the Moon has been worshipped for millennia as a Goddess because menstruation and fertility in humans was understood as synchronous with the *lunation cycle* of 29½ days. There are even sculptures dating back beyond the last Ice Age which confirm this numerically, like the famous *Venus of Laussal*.

Tides are also linked to the lunation cycle; anyone living an outdoor existence near to the coast will quickly connect the state of the tide with the *position* of the Moon in the sky. High tides always occurs when the Moon is at one of two *opposite* positions during the day; one of these is above, and the other below, the local horizon and they are fixed for a particular location. As the tides are synchronized to the lunar 'day' of 24 hours and 48 minutes, knowledge of the *position* of the Moon enables one to know the state of the sea-tide, and also to know whether the tide is ebbing or flowing. In addition, knowing the *phase* of the Moon enables a latter-day astronomer-priest to predict whether it will be a high 'spring' tide or a shallow range 'neap' tide, and whether high tide will occur in the morning or afternoon.

This kind of knowledge is considered worthless today, but such was not always the case. In some of the oldest texts from the Celtic monasteries and colleges, we can read that such knowledge was once considered vital to an educated person. The epigram poem *Saltair Na Rann* dates from the tenth century CE, although its roots may be traced back far earlier. It itemizes five essential items of knowledge required by 'every understanding person' in holy orders,

For each day five items of knowledge
Are required for every understanding person
From everyone, without appearance of boasting
who is in holy orders.

The day of the solar month; the age of the Moon
The state of the sea-tide, without error;
The day of the week; the calendar of the feasts of the perfect saints
In just clarity with their variations.

Here we have a clear statement that Celtic monks were required to understand the basic motions and cycles of the Sun and Moon – a direct legacy from the megalith builders. Perhaps we might not be surprised at this apparent continuity, for the traditions of the circle builders must have permeated down into the Celtic culture, and this region of the world was where the astronomy of the Sun and Moon had apparently been established long before any other known culture had grappled with its complexities. This particular legacy of the megalith builders is once more becoming available to every 'understanding person' and it is clear that astronomical considerations formed part of the design of many sites. It is now known that the human body synchronizes to the lunar day and not the solar day when placed in sensory deprivation – places where the diurnal light rhythm is excluded. Such conditions exist deep inside the initiatory burial chambers of Newgrange in the Boyne Valley, Ireland and elsewhere.

Sticks and stones – how to preserve culture for 5,000 years

It is important to recognize that wooden posts make perfectly adequate sighting poles for alignments to rising and setting celestial bodies. Posts would be more accurate than stone in many cases, certainly much easier to transport and position, although there would be little evidence left of a 5,000-year-old wooden-post structure today. The need to build geometric structures in stone is astronomically unnecessary and suggests an over-riding ceremonial and ritual function for the use of stone. It also informs us how to successfully preserve a cultural message for 5,000 years – 50 tonne stones *endure*.

A visitor to stone circles needs to remember that what is seen today is often not what was erected originally. Erosion, damage, vandalism and even the rotting of all non-stone structures present a lop-sided

picture of how the site might have appeared when it was built. Many circles were built around existing wooden-post structures. The original number of stones is not always the number we count today – stones were systematically removed and used for mill grinding-wheels, building stone, lintels and gate-posts. Cairns of small stones in the centre or on the bank of an original henge are easily moved by children at play and displaced by animals. Earthen mounds covering cist burials have often been eroded and washed out to extinction by rain. Wooden structures have long since rotted away, leaving such scant traces in their post holes that even archaeologists are often hard pressed to locate, identify and date their residual deposits. The huge wooden halls erected by the Celts during the Dark Ages within henges (Tara in Eire and Castle Dore in Cornwall) have left almost no traces after just 1,400 years.

Although there is a strong suspicion that the early stone circles (before 2700 BCE) were connected with henges, the two structures, like the wooden 'halls', may not have been built at the same time. Nowhere may this be demonstrated more clearly than in the various 'phases' of Stonehenge. The henge ditch and bank, the early wooden structure at the centre, the sarsen circle, the original wooden circle, the bluestone circle(s), the trilithon ellipse and the 56-hole Aubrey circle represent a 1,600-year evolutionary period for this monument. Stonehenge is now a ruined *collage* of a completed evolutionary process in time and space (Figure 2.2). Many other circles may have enjoyed a similar evolution of design, function and adaptation; the stones are the bones of what once must have been a complex human social artefact.

Cultural continuity and sacred geometry

A modern map showing the location of stone circles (Figure 2.1) is also a collage of at least three distinct periods identified within the European circle building tradition.

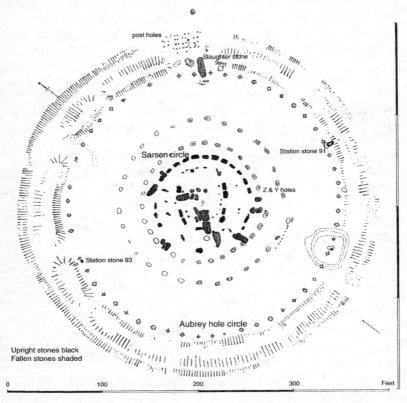

post holes

Slaughter stone

Sarsen circle

Station stone 91

Z & Y holes

Station stone 93

Aubrey hole circle

Upright stones black
Fallen stones shaded

| 0 | 100 | 200 | 300 | Feet |

Figure 2.2 Plan view of Stonehenge. The chronology 'implodes' from the Aubrey circle (circa 3100 BCE) to the inner bluestone horseshoe (circa 1500 BCE).

The middle to late neolithic circles are mainly to be found in the northern half of the United Kingdom and Ireland and date from about 3400 to 2700 BCE. Then the late Neolithic to early Bronze Age circles, scattered liberally throughout the United Kingdom with concentrations in Cornwall and Brittany, date from 2700 BCE to about 2000 BCE. The most prolific period for the art of stone circle building was the 'late period' from 2000 BCE to 1200 BCE, the middle

Bronze Age, which was chiefly concentrated in Scotland. After this period, few circles were erected and, importantly, none are known from later than 1000 BCE.

Despite this separation in time, the complex geometries of some of the flattened circles, egg-shaped rings and ellipses built throughout the entire period were identical and were built in all regions. There is, therefore, no doubt that the technique for laying out the site and marking it was a continuous cultural 'artefact', as were the technological aids required. Non-elastic rope of hemp or nettle together with pegs formed the 'hardware', whilst the geometric techniques to divide a line, create a right angle or a long accurate straight line, re-proportion a line and create multiple radius arcs were the cultural 'software' of the architects throughout the whole period of circle building. But how were the building instructions stored?

This information was somehow passed down from generation to generation as also it was diffused amongst the entire region. Even the favoured unit of length – the *Megalithic yard* – was transmitted throughout the whole region and throughout the whole period. How was this achieved? Roughly, the Megalithic yard is a human pace. Two MY form a *Megalithic fathom*, and this is approximately the distance between finger tip to finger tip across the arms of an average human span; 2.5 MY is also commonly found and became known as the *Megalithic rod*.

The place of the dead

There has always been, in the words of William Stukeley, in describing stone circles, 'an uninterrupted tradition of their being sacred'. Death and stone circles are irrevocably linked, and there were multiple burials and cremation pits at many sites. Many of these are found at astronomically salient places within a stone ring – especially near extreme rising and setting positions of the Moon. Although archaeologists are not in agreement as to the usefulness of assuming that the burials were contemporary to possible other

functions of the circle, the bones and cremations tell us that the enclosed space formed by the circle was sacred in some way, and often appears connected to celestial events.

The remains of children have been found in henge banks and within stone circles, with suggestions that these may have been ritual sacrifices. Burials have been found where arrowheads may be seen lodged within the vertebrae of the spine. Fragments of many smashed skulls, half skeletons and mutilated skeletons have also been found within a grisly catalogue of excavated remains whose implications many in our modern world would rather not face. Dr Aubrey Burl suggests that,

> The most likely explanation for these bizarre collections of bones, some of them lacking skulls and far too few to represent even a minute fraction of the population, is that they were the remains of an ancestor cult in which the living ritually used skulls and longbones, believing that the ghosts of the dead would protect them just as dedicatory burial would add potency to a ceremonial monument. In the new stone age death and the dead obsessed the living. But, needing to control these powerful and dangerous spirits, the people confined the bones inside 'magic' rings of earth or stone.

We cannot refute or ignore this kind of evidence, however much some New Age authors seek to present our 'druidic' and 'pagan' forebears as superwise, compassionate versions of ourselves, Pythagoras or astronomer Patrick Moore. The projection of our own cultural values on to the past is never going to unlock the culture of the megalith builders, which certainly appears to have included ritual sacrifice at certain times. Horrible to us, sure, but our present culture still sanctions the killing of miscreants, and the mass murders at Auschwitz and other concentration camps occurred in the *twentieth* century. Unless one knows the circumstances which led to the deaths at stone circles, it is very, very hard to make a judgement on the social context from a few bone flakes, although one cannot help but be touched at a 5,000-year-old internment ceremony which included flowers, shells, quartz crystals and a delicate arranging of the body into a foetal position aligned to the

rising Sun, with food pots and other worldly goods lain alongside to accompany the traveller on her journey to the Otherworld and, one might assume, rebirth.

Our culture is frightened by death and has broken the circle of connection between death and rebirth. Our traditional religion is an import, one of just a few belief systems in the world which espouse the concept of a 'one-shot' life followed by either eternal heaven or eternal hell. There can be and were other cultural views concerning life after death. Neolithic and Bronze Age people clearly saw a relevance in having the bones or cremated remains of certain ancestors buried in a sacred space, available for consultation and for warding off evil within the sacred space of the tribe. By definition, those bones were confirmation that the tribe had *survived*, this alone would have provided a sense of security within the culture, and a right to ownership of the immediate surrounding territory. Perhaps they were the bones of an elite group – the leaders of the tribe.

The gathering of the tribe

A main plank in the archaeological evidence states that circles were places of communal meetings and ritual ceremony – a kind of megalithic circus ring, church, market square or council chamber. There is much evidence to support this view at many sites. Some circles have paved or cobbled interiors, and many have clearly marked 'entrances', with grandiose multiple stone portals to mark the point of entry. The distribution of stone rings in some regions suggest a strong territorial or tribal purpose. For example, in north-east Scotland, every 13 square kilometres (5 square miles) or so, one finds similar designs of ring where a huge recumbant stone faces the southern moonset. Quartz chippings were scattered around this stone as if to emphasize the lunar connection, and cupmarks bored into its surface mark and align with stages in the lunar 18.6-year cycle. These circles form a localized design type – with ten or eleven stones forming a circle with the recumbant stone and its flanking stones. In Pembrokeshire, near the northern coastline, a

similar distribution of burial cromlechs strongly suggests a territorial basis for this placement. 'This is our land because all our ancestors lived and are buried here' as one book succinctly puts it. [*Neolithic Sites in Cardiganshire, Carmarthanshire and Pembrokeshire* by George Nash and George Children, published by Logaston Press ISBN 1-873827-997.]

If we are safe in assuming a link between quartz and the Moon, then it is easy to suggest one function of adjacent quartz boulders which clearly show the way to many circles. In Wales, huge quartz boulders mark crossroads and ancient trackways as well as stone circles, and it is sensible to suggest that these white ghosts of the hedgerows, reflecting the light from the Moon, serve a practical, in addition to any possible esoteric, purpose for those wishing to navigate at night in an age before moonlight had been replaced by streetlights and torches. Quartz was neolithic cat's-eyes, if you like.

Other factors to be considered at stone circle sites are the 'cup and ring' marks, spirals and chevron designs sometimes carved on an important stone. Megalithic art remains to be properly understood, although it is hard not to see repeated patterns of lunar and calendraic numbers within many of the designs (Figure 2.3). Some researchers recognize similarities between the spiral and labyrinthine designs and those found in ceremonies of initiation and ritual by tribal peoples today. The suggestion that megalithic sites were places of initiation, perhaps involving drug-induced states of consciousness, has enjoyed wide appeal amongst today's modern drug-aware culture. However seductive certain New Age publishers package this concept, no mention is ever made of the ritual sacrifice aspects which many have accompanied the drugs. In addition, we hear little about the dreadfully short life expectancy of adults during this era, nor the horrid catalogue of diseases to which they fell prone. The archaeological evidence on these matters cannot be questioned merely because it spoils any illusions about a Golden Age. Unless this evidence is one day shown to be incorrect, then life for our circle builders was probably quite an ordeal.

It is not possible for us to recreate the ceremonies or rituals of the circle builders, nor is it easy to understand their mindset. All the

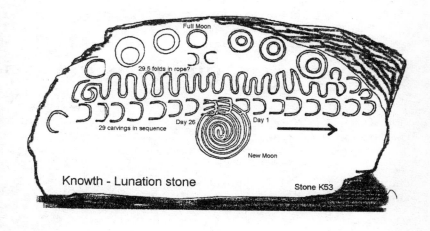

Figure 2.3 The lunation cycle inscribed in stone circa 3200 BCE

modern student of such things can do is to be accepting and tolerant of many widespread theories from archaeologists, astronomers, geometers, engineers, leyhunters, anthropologists, dowsers, folklorists, mythologists, theologists, shamans and priests. Somewhere, within all of these disciplines, may lurk the answers we seek.

However, we can avoid making one common error. We must not assume that megalithic people were any less than ourselves in their ability to *think*. Modern anthropology and science had shown that humans have remained intellectually much as they are today since about 100,000 BCE. We use the word *neanderthal* to describe stupid and gross people, thus confirming our prejudice and ignorance towards other cultures, in this case *homo sapiens neaderthalensis* and its culture – which survived far longer than our present one to date. Our cartoons depict Stone Age man as a near-ape doing near-ape tasks. Until quite recently, similar cartoons could be commonly

found depicting Black and Asian people in the same way; our culture has had to recognize how inaccurate, intolerant and offensive such material is, and what fears it masks in our present culture. Perhaps it is high time we did the same for our megalithic ancestors.

The astronomic connection

The alignment of stone circles to astronomical risings and settings is another well-trodden route by which a function for these enigmatic constructions may be suggested. Yet, while a great number of impressive megalithic sites contain clear evidence of alignments to key solar and lunar rising and setting positions, many do not. But many circles are clearly and obviously 'plugged in' to their local sky patterns.

Astronomical sightlines were an integral part of the design of many sites. Indeed, because sites appear to be connected with rituals concerned with the treatment of the dead, we can immediately suggest that any burial aligned to north, south, east or west, has to be undertaken using a knowledge of basic astronomy – for how else can these cardinal points of the compass be determined? Thus, events in the sky and the treatment of the dead are shown to be connected, and this is an important link.

Ever since William Stukeley noted that Stonehenge was aligned to the summer solstice sunrise, the megaliths have been shown to be linked with astronomy. The megalith builders were as interested in the extreme motions of the Moon as they were in those of the Sun. Alignments to the key stations of the Moon through her 18.6-year cycle are commonly met alongside those to the solstitial and equinoctial sunrises and sunsets. All along the west coast of Brittany, Cornwall, Wales, the English Lakes and western Scotland, the elevated coastal terrain supports a fine view to a distant sea horizon, and it is here that one may most commonly find alignments of stones marking the key stations of both the setting Sun and Moon. In Brittany, distant islands off the coast have strategically placed standing stones which act as foresights to these megalithic sites,

providing rifle-barrel accuracy. The azimuth angles of the key positions of the Sun and Moon change with latitude and the reader can find these angles in Table 6.1, for various latitudes from Brittany to Orkney.

We may never know quite how adept this culture was at understanding the sky. What we can now appreciate is that their original alignments were so accurate that they can sometimes be used to date a site to within a century or so, by taking account of the known reduction in the Earth's axial tilt angle and its effects on the extreme rising and setting angles of the Sun and Moon. The scores of alignments to hill and mountain tops, notches in distant horizons and suitably placed standing stones indicate a culture which was doing accurate astronomy by observing angles of rise and set against the horizon to a few minutes of a degree and had understood the major cycles of the Sun and Moon. (See Chapter 6).

The geometry of stone circles

Since the surveys of Alex Thom provided researchers with accurate plans of hundreds of sites, at least seven clearly defined geometries emerge from within the corpus of surviving rings. These geometries are described later in this book and provide much evidence that number and geometry played a vital role in the cultural paradigm of these people. The division of a circle into equally spaced parts is demonstrated at site after site, together with proof that this culture was technically proficient at marking out a site using ropes and pegs to high accuracies. These astronomer-priests could divide a line into equal parts, bisect an angle, construct a perpendicular to a line, reproportion a line, work with Pythagorean triangles, whole number ratios and a lot more. Whilst the evidence is doubted by some, the sites are themselves testimony to these things, once they are measured with sufficient accuracy. Unbelievably, we never did that until quite recently.

Summary

The building of a stone circle involved complex factors and reasons, some of which were related to geometry, some to astronomy and some to the treatment of the dead and other essential social functions within this remarkable culture. Today, what you believe together with your background in this subject will invariably determine what you experience when you visit a stone circle. This is a common enough phenomenon when dealing with an unknown object – one projects preconceived notions on to it in order to test whether anything in one's past experiences fits the new situation. It is a confirmation of the alien nature of the megalithic culture compared to our own that so many people project their emotional needs, fantasies and theories concerning the past on to these innocent circles. In a later chapter we will study the reasons for this and explore the different motives which draw people to these relics from the past.

THE PATTERNS
OF THE PAST

A Geomancy Primer I

*We first demonstrate that there is a presumption amounting to a
certainty that a definite unit was used in setting out these rings.
It is proposed to call this the Megalithic yard ... It will appear
that the Megalithic yard is 2.72 ft.*

Alexander Thom, *Megalithic Sites in Britain* (Oxford
University Press, 1967, page 36)

The culture or cultures that built stone circles left us no plans or
written accounts of their motives nor reasons for their prolific
output of complex geometric designs. Until the twentieth century, no
one even guessed that these constructions were, in fact, often not
circles at all. If an archaeologist noticed departure from circularity,
the model of ancient culture held by them merely led to the
conclusion that the shape was a 'failed circle', confirming the
primitive nature of megalithic society. This was an understandable
though terrible mistake, and this kind of circular and self-fulfilling
argument was not at all scientific and helped perpetuate belief in the
primitive status of the circle builders.

Viewed from the ground, it is usually hard to notice any departure
from circularity in stone rings. Once we dispel the 'failed circle'
hypothesis, we are bidden to accept that the geometry of these sites
was extremely accurately defined and vitally important to the
builders, although perhaps not for the later users of the site.

Sufficient well-preserved circles existed for Alex Thom to accurately survey hundreds of examples. Shortly after the Second World War, the Thom family made circle visiting and measuring their vocational calling. In a fine old shooting brake, they lugged theodolites and surveyor's chains up mountains and across bog and gorse-spraked scrubland. The astonishing results of these arduous labours meant that, by the mid-1960s, Thom possessed a 'well constructed parcel bomb', which he then dropped through the letterbox of the archaeological establishment.

Thoms conclusions were scientific, he had been Professor Emeritus of Engineering at Oxford. His conclusions were practical and realistic; he was a lifelong amateur astronomer and an expert in astro-navigation and surveying. Alex Thom was no armchair theorist nor, by any manner of speaking, a member of the New Age. His conclusions, listed in Table 3.1, are to be found in his book, *Megalithic Sites in Britain* (Oxford University Press 1967, ISBN 0 19 813148 8).

Table 3.1 Thom's conclusions about stone circles and their builders

> 1 The megalithic architects were using a standard unit of length – which Thom called the *Megalithic yard* (MY) – whose length was 2.72 feet (0.83 m or 32.63 inches) in length. Using a rigorous statistical analysis based on over 100 circles, the tolerance range for the MY suggested a deviation in length within an astonishing 0.003 feet. Thom suggested that the measuring rods used by the builders were issued from a central source.
> 2 Many standing stones and stone circles incorporated alignments to key solar and lunar risings and settings. These alignments often utilized a natural foresight such as a mountain feature many tens of miles away, offering angular resolution down to a few minutes of a degree.
> 3 Many megalithic sites were using alignments to certain favoured fixed stars, notably Deneb, Capella and Altair. Because their rising and setting positions change very slowly with the precessional shift of the Earth, Thom thereby was able to estimate the constructional date of the circle or standing stone involved. At the time, dating derived from this technique appeared far too early,

but only because the faults inherent within the early carbon dating process had not been identified.

4 The builders tended to use *whole numbers* or half numbers of MY in their radii. In their perimeter lengths there was a preference for multiples of 2.5 MY, a length which Thom termed the *Megalithic rod*.

5 The stones were placed with their *centres* on the line of the intended and marked-out geometry.

6 The geometry of many non-circular rings was not due to haphazard constructional techniques; there were many consistent geometries reproduced throughout the whole megalithic region and these involved flattened arcs, the use of whole-number Pythagorean triangles and multiple foci.

Archaeologists behaving badly

As a retired academic himself, Thom might have guessed at the reaction all this would have had on archaeologists – the silence from their quarters was deafening! Most of them ignored his conclusions completely – it simply didn't fit that ancient Britons were skilled at Pythagorean geometry, nor that their culture was capable of standardizing and maintaining a unit of length to within 0.1 per cent throughout the land for over two millennia. Some archaeologists treated the retired professor shamefully, although this failed to daunt 'Sandy' Thom one jot. In an interview with journalist and broadcaster Magnus Magnusson, when asked, 'Your theories about Stone Age Einsteins have got up the nose of some archeologists. The idea that the cup and ring marks were used as writing has got up the backs of a lot more. Does it worry you?', Thom replied, with a laugh, 'Not in the slightest, I just go right on … recording what I find'. [*Chronicle*, BBC, autumn 1969.]

Things changed little in Thom's remaining years, although the foremost authority on Stonehenge, the late professor Richard Atkinson, was honest enough to come across to Thom's side on more than one public occasion and to admit that he had been wrong in initially condemning Thom's work. Indeed, they colluded on the most accurate survey plan of Stonehenge to date. Now, 30 years on, some establishment authors are including the Megalithic yard and other conclusions from Thom's work within their theses and textbooks. In archaeology, the mills of change grind very slowly.

A REALISTIC TECHNOLOGY

We must now look at the technology available to the circle builders as evidenced by the remarkable accuracy of their work. All of their constructions may be geometrically replicated on a beach or flattish field using just pegs and ropes. Because I have found this is a good way to approach the megalithic mindset, I have incorporated practical exercises within this inventory of techniques, and the interested reader is invited to prepare the items in Table 3.2 in advance. All this kit, bar the rods, should fit inside a smallish rucksack, and is not too heavy to trundle about. Much of this material will be useful when making visits to actual megalithic sites.

Table 3.2 Equipment list to mark out and replicate the geometry of known stone circle designs

1 A long length of non-stretchy rope, about 50 MY (40 m; 44 yards) in length and accurately marked in Megalithic yards. You can define any unit of length you wish, but for reasons explained later, it would be good to choose the pre-metric foot (12 inches or 0.33 m) or the Megalithic yard. You may use other units of length, but the rope will then be less useful in later chapters. Ensure that the lengths are equal and derived from a standard length. I use a length of dowel exactly one MY in length (32.63 inches or 82.9 cms) to check this. Place small loops of nylon monofilament (fishing line is ideal) at every MY

along the length – this is harder than you think to do accurately, and I colour code these nylon rope 'tags'. Alternatively, they can loop through plastic plant labels, which are inexpensive, to assist counting and minimize the chances of error. Red fluorescent ('day-glo') paint is excellent for visibility in grass or on a sandy beach. As a refinement, you can usefully mark the half MY points.

2 Obtain some metal tent pegs or whittle some wooden pegs with sharp points on one end. You will need perhaps 20 of these, together with a mallet for driving them into the ground.

3 A metal tape or a surveyor's cloth tape measure is useful for checking accuracies.

4 A set of six or eight 3-foot poles, sharpened at one end and preferably striped alternately day-glo red and white. Some striped in MY, others in feet, for reasons which will become apparent later.

5 Lots of heavy duty elastic bands to hold the poles together.

6 A magnetic compass and a pocket calculator.

You can now embark on *exactly* the same design routes as our megalithic forebears undertook over 4,000 years ago – for apparently there is no other way to reproduce these shapes. There are no prizes for high accuracy, but you should establish the principles of each design and understand the design route if you want to understand this culture a little better.

Geomancy is the science (and art) of laying out shapes on the landscape. In ancient times, several cultures developed this to a fine art, such as the Nazca people in Peru, the temple builders of the Egyptians and Greeks, the Mayans, the Knights Templar and, perhaps first of all, the European megalith builders, who are our concern here.

Tbe Leyline problem

Any Ordnance Survey or small-scale map will show you that ancient sites sometimes appear to form alignments, as part of a network of ancient sites. These alignments are today often called *leys* or *leylines*,

and they are actually quite contentious, because the cultural implications of admitting their existence requires that our history books are all rewritten. Open-minded historians ask how and why ancient people had the skills to arrange for their artefacts to lie on straight lines over vast distances across the landscape, these including holy wells, springs, tumuli, mounds, bridges, crossroads, churches and natural features such as notches in hill-tops. Others declare them as the bogus inventions of leyhunters and many people refuse to accept that leys are other than a coincidence. You can decide this for yourself, but only after studying maps, visiting sites and attempting exercise one! It may also help to read *Earth Mysteries – a beginner's guide*, by Teresa Moorey, in this series of books.

Many of the features on apparent leylines are not connected in the same historical time frame and, sometimes, the alignments are not exact. This isn't the problem many sceptics make it, nor does it debunk every aspect of the leyline hypothesis. Churches are often 2,000 or 3,000 years more recent than a tumulus or holy well, yet we have already discovered that the early Church Fathers ordered churches to be built on ancient sacred sites. They were to be incorporated within the older architecture of the megalithic culture. This is why leys include later Christian architecture within their alignments. Modern bridges are also often built on the site of an ancient bridge or ford, simply because this is the only suitable place along a certain stretch of river bank.

The discoverer of leys, Alfred Watkins, thought he had found an ancient matrix of connections between ancient sites. In a revelation, he saw his local landscape in Herefordshire linked by a complex network of lines which connected churches, moats, castles, hill-tops, bridges, fords, farm gates, crossroads and ancient sites such as standing stones and stone circles. Afterwards, in 1925, Watkins wrote his book, *The Old Straight Track*, which is still the reference and starting point for many leyhunters worldwide.

Whilst leylines remain contentious, the work of certain researchers has usefully pushed back some of the fog which surrounds the subject. Hamish Miller and Paul Broadhurst's book, *The Sun and the Serpent*, may be heartily recommended for this purpose, although, generally, what many New Age authors write about leylines is

entirely subjective – the very word *leyline* can now mean almost anything. The reader may be assured that the alignments referred to in this book remain, whatever else they may prove to become or incorporate in the coming years, straight lines across the landscape laid out by ancient people using known technology.

Alignments – making straight lines

Alignments from stone circles to other sites can be found, to remarkable accuracy, and many stone circles lie on alignments or tangentially to them. To begin our understanding of ancient geomancy, let's look at how a line on the landscape – an *alignment* – can be made, using only neolithic equipment.

Long, straight lines are not difficult to make, although extremely accurate alignments over many miles demand an experienced hand, eye and brain. Surveyors still use aligned rods to establish alignments, and the old 'dodman' with his two sticks may still be found within our legends and even cut into chalk downland as *The Long Man of*

Figure 3.1 The Long Man of Wilmington. The 'dodsticks' become parallel and the proportions become human when viewed from 76 metres (250 feet) above Wilmington Church. Courtesy Rodney Castleden.

33

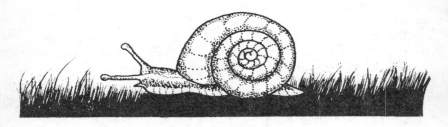

Figure 3.2 Snail with 'dod-sticks'. In olden times snails were called 'dods'.

Wilmington in Sussex (Figure 3.1). In rural areas, snails are still sometimes called 'dods' because their two eye-stalks resemble dod-sticks or surveyor's poles (Figure 3.2).

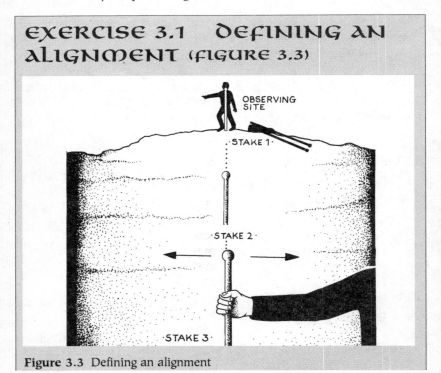

EXERCISE 3.1   DEFINING AN ALIGNMENT (FIGURE 3.3)

OBSERVING SITE

·STAKE 1·

·STAKE 2·

·STAKE 3·

Figure 3.3 Defining an alignment

Find a high spot on the local landscape and locate your house or some other notable feature from it. Leaving a friend to remain on the summit, take a set of long poles (canes are just about fine) and, every so often, push one into the ground so that it stands vertical and is in the alignment. Your friend will be able to shout 'left'! or 'right!' for about half a mile, thereafter you'll need body language, a flashlight, mobile phones or CB radios. These latter two are hardly neolithic, and are therefore to be discouraged as cheating! Eventually, three or four poles will describe the direction from the high spot to your point of reference.

You could now try measuring the angle from north using a compass. This is called the *azimuth* or bearing. Magnetic compasses are also not standard neolithic issue and, even worse, they do not point to true north (In Britain, the reading would be about four degrees 'out', to the west of north). To find true north, *one must take observations of the sky – 'read' it* (Table 3.2).

Table 3.2 True north may be found in several ways:

1 All objects in the sky, stars, planets and the Sun and Moon, culminate directly south of an observer. The Sun culminates at local noon, and *only then* does a shadow cast by a vertical stick make a north–south line (Figure 3.4a). The problem is, that clock time oscillates around this position through the year, so that errors of many degrees can be made when this oscillation is at a peak. A graph of the correction needed is given in Figure 3.4b.
   In Britain, local noon may easily be found (to within a degree) by remembering that one degree of longitude is equivalent to a four-minute change from the clock time. Add for west longitude, subtract for east longitude. Thus, if you live in Buxton, Derbyshire, (two degrees west), then local noon is eight minutes after noon (or 1:08 p.m. if Summer Time is in force). If you live near Colchester, Essex, (one degree east) then local noon is at 11:56 a.m. (12:56 p.m. if Summer Time is in force). Refer to your local Ordnance Survey map to determine the longitude of your

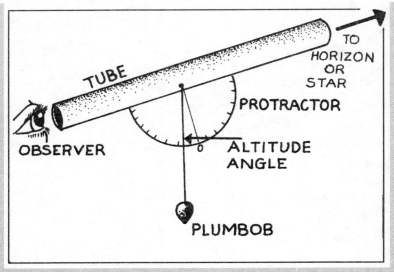

Figure 3.4a A simple clinometer

location and then work out four minutes of time per degree. Finally, apply the correction in Figure 3.4b, and you will have your north–south line to within a degree.

Having found true north, it is then possible to place a north–south row of stakes, just as you did for the alignment from the high place to your point of reference. You can then establish the *azimuth angle* of your alignment from point of reference to the high place. The *azimuth bearing* of a site is its angle from where you are standing measured clockwise from true north. You may now cheat and compare your measured angle with that taken from the OS map. You will find that it is hard to determine this angle to an accuracy of better than one degree, even with a protractor to help you.

2 The pole star lies within a degree of true north. Its altitude angle gives the latitude of the location directly, again to within a degree. A *clinometer* is useful for making this measurement (Figure 3.4a).

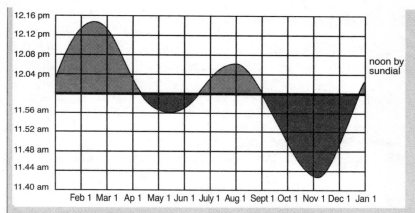

Figure 3.4b Corrections to sundial or 'shadow stick' noon

The alignment you have made should enable you and a friend to develop a deep respect for the megalithic architects, who laid out some of their constructions to well within a degree and some of their alignments to within a few minutes of a degree. You have now established an observing platform, and can use these same techniques to find the directions of key landmarks from there, using your hard-won north–south line to measure the angle.

Seen from your point of reference, the high spot will not be on the actual horizon, it will have an *altitude*. The altitude of a site is simply the angle from the horizontal by which you must crank your eyeballs up and down in order to locate the site and a clinometer can measure this angle. If you live in a mountainous region, this angle may be over 30 degrees; while in a generally flat landscape it may be less than a degree.

Every identified landmark around your chosen site may now be identified by just two angles; an azimuth bearing and a horizon altitude. Thus, from my site, the mountain peak of *Carn Ingli* is at azimuth 235° and altitude 1° 30′. For future use, you should attempt to describe in this way at least ten or twelve landmarks around the local horizon from your chosen high spot. These first few landmarks will assist in the later process of understanding the calendar date from the yearly cycle of sunrises and sunsets.

Megalithic Stone Rows

Megalithic surveyors commonly made two principal types of alignment. The first involved watching a rising or setting celestial object (a fixed star, or the Sun or Moon rising or setting on an equinox, solstice or 'lunstice'). A point on the horizon such as a notch in a distant mountain-top defined the alignment angle and, to confirm it or draw attention to it, a stone or chain was placed in line from a defined observing place. Kintraw in Scotland is certainly such a case. A cobbled platform near to a cairn and a standing stone

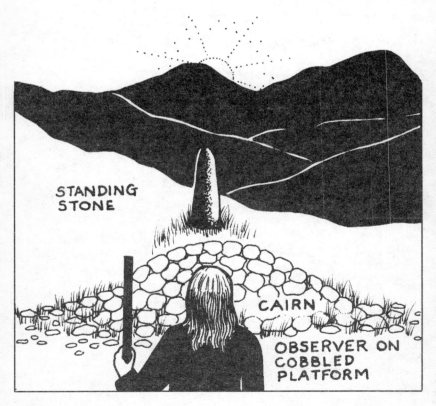

Figure 3.5 The Kintraw winter solstice alignment

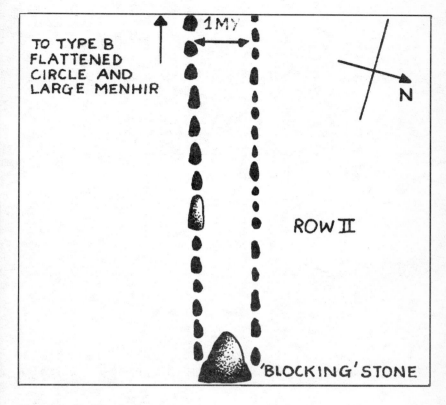

TO TYPE B
FLATTENED
CIRCLE AND
LARGE MENHIR

1MY

ROW II

N

'BLOCKING' STONE

Figure 3.6a Merrivale stone rows

(unfortunately toppled in 1972) leads the eye to the distant mountains where the Sun slides down the side of a mountain *only* at the winter solstice (Figure 3.5).

The second type of alignment is defined by a set of stones, cairns or other features arranged in straight rows. An intended astronomical alignment may or may not also be present. *Merrivale* on Dartmoor is perhaps the best-known site – here, two stone rows angled at just over 2 degrees from parallel stretch from west to east for over half a mile (Figure 3.6a). In Wales, *Parc y Meirw* ('The Place of the Dead')

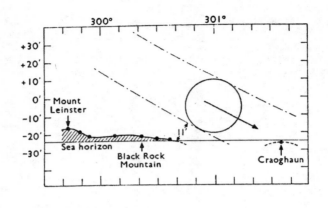

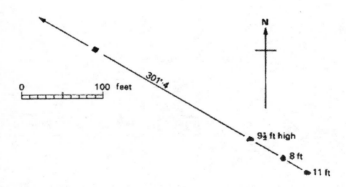

Figure 3.6b Parc y Meirw ('The place of the dead')

combined five stones in a row aligned to a distant Irish mountain-top (over 70 miles away) marking the minor standstill setting of the Moon (Figure 3.6b). *Nine Maidens* in Cornwall comprises nine large stones aligned to the rising of the fixed star Deneb (Figure 3.6c). These sites,

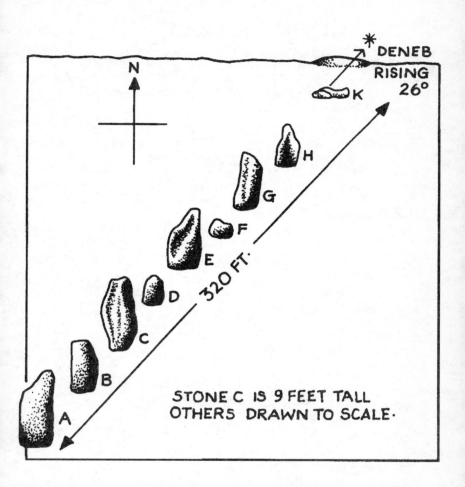

Figure 3.6c Nine Maidens

and scores of other examples, prove the case that megalithic people had mastered the art of arranging linear features on the landscape to high accuracies for astronomical reasons. But did they use and understand other shapes?

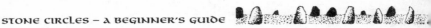

TRIANGLES

During the construction of several of the more common shapes of stone ring, the builders would have been led to both construct and wrestle with the properties of triangles, particularly right-angled triangles (see later).

EXERCISE 3.2 GEOMANCY – THE CONSTRUCTION OF A RIGHT ANGLE USING ROPES AND PEGS

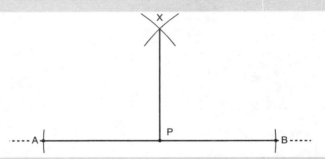

Figure 3.7 Constructing a right angle at P on an alignment

This technique can be understood in seconds and then mastered over a lifetime (Figure 3.7).

Rope marked with equal lengths can also be used to produce a right angle, but only with certain combinations of side lengths; 3:4:5 and 5:12:13 are both 'Pythagoren' right-angled triangles to be found at megalithic sites, as are the less practically useful 12:35:37 and the less accurate 7:7:10. The 3:4:5 triangle is made from a rope which contains 13 knots marking 12 lengths and is called, probably inaccurately, a *Druid's Cord.* These triangles are shown in Figure 3.8.

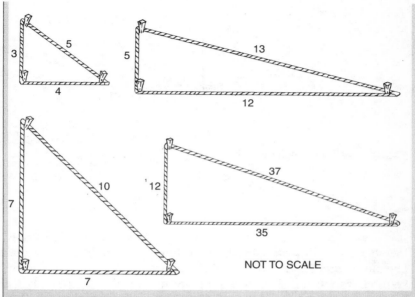

Figure 3.8 Pythagorean triangles

EXERCISE 3.3

Peg out a right angle using all four of the above triangles. Can you measure the departure from a right angle in the 7:7:10?

BISECTING A LINE

The technique to divide a line into two involves a slight modification of that used to construct a right angle, and is shown with it (Figure 3.9).

OTHER LINEAR SHAPES

Later in this chapter we will find evidence to connect megalithic surveyors with complex linear shapes within circles. Cue for some curvy work!

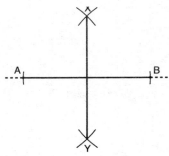

Figure 3.9 Bisecting the line *AB*

Circles

It is easy to make a circle and the technology to do so is as equally low-tech as that for straight lines and triangles. A marked rope and a peg are all that is needed to define a centre, then a brief walk from centre to radius followed by a stroll around a circular perimeter is all that it takes. It requires little intelligence to make a circle and a lot of experience to make an accurate one. Every raindrop makes a circle when it falls into a puddle, but the circle doesn't last and it is not a fixed size. For that, one needs a rope and peg, and it is better if the rope doesn't stretch and even better still if the perimeter can be accurately marked on the ground as the rope is taken around it.

EXERCISE 3.4   MAKING CIRCLES

Find a level surface. A beach or recreational park is ideal, although a flat floor or large piece of paper mounted on an unfolded corrugated cardboard box is suitable too.

I have always found that the best circles are made in the following way. Loop the rope around a peg driven into the intended centre of the circle. A loop is the best way, because then the loop 'walks' easily around the peg as you scribe the perimeter. At the other end of the loop, whose length defines the

radius of the circle, a sharp scribing peg is used to scratch the turf or sand (Figure 3.10). On paper or a flat floor, a pencil or chalk marker must be used. The perimeter may now be traced and the circle completed. For an outdoor circle, white quartz pebbles, flour, sand or sawdust may be used to define the circle – even 50-tonne stones if you feel a megalithic mood coming on!

ROPE LOOP

POINTED STAKE

CENTRAL STAKE

Figure 3.10 Marking out a circle: flour, sawdust or pebbles may be used to mark the perimeter

For a first circle, I'd recommend a radius about 7 MY. Tie a large loop of 14 MY in the marked rope so that placed over the peg and pulled taut, the other end of the loop defines the desired radius (7 MY). Now take one of the long poles and, keeping it *as vertical as you can*, use it like a pen – scratching the turf or sand to mark the perimeter. Small pegs driven into the perimeter every few MY can define the circle perimeter as you progress, which is where a friend once more comes in handy. Circle building is a gregarious activity.

PI IN THE SKY

Another interesting exercise is to lay a rope around the perimeter and then compare its length to the radius. If you do this accurately, you will find that you can fit three diameters plus about a seventh of a diameter into the perimeter. The exact number cannot be found – it is an irrational number, *pi*, whose approximate value is 22/7 or, more accurately, 3.14159265… You can never know the exact value of *pi* although, practically, you can get very near.

EXERCISE 3.5   TO MEASURE 'PI' QUITE ACCURATELY

Lay the marked rope around the perimeter and then count the length. Divide this by the length of the original loop and the result should be a little more than 3. Some students can obtain 22/7 by using the suggested 7 MY radius. You may like to think about the whole number (integer) value of radius which would furnish an integer value for the circumference. I am sure megalithic folk wrestled with this kind of problem.

In making a circle this way you are copying *exactly* the techniques used by our circle-building ancestors over 4,000 years ago, and they had no trouble building thousands of circles, often in very inaccessible places. Some circles have diameters of over 90 metres (300 feet). Megalithic people also trundled huge stones, often over many miles, to define the perimeters of their circles – so these constructions must have been very important to their culture.

THE PROBLEM OF LARGER CIRCLES

If marking your stone circle appears relatively easy, then how would you lay out a circle having a radius measured in miles? It appears

that our ancient geomancers solved this problem, as covered in David Furlong's book, *The Keys to the Temple*, where he proposes two huge circular 'leys' in Wiltshire. As a former surveyor himself, David quickly spotted the astonishing accuracies in the arrangement of so many features on the perimeter of a circle. Rope and pegs from the centre are here not adequate to explain the feature (Figure 3.11).

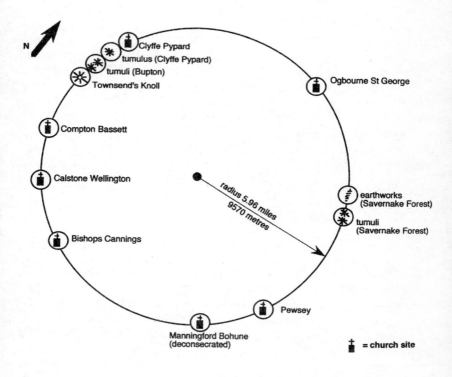

Figure 3.11 A circular 'ley'. The western circle investigated by David Furlong

The year, the month and the day drawn out

The circle perimeter represents eternity – it has no beginning and no ending. This is a concept worth thinking about, for a glimpse of infinity may be had by standing in the middle of your circle and pointing in any direction. If you move your pointed finger around the full circle, then in that single act, you have also pointed your way around the entire universe. The centre is the Earth and *all our cycles of time fit into this circle*. The *year* (365.242 days) is the time it takes the Sun to (apparently) move around the zodiac, the *sidereal month* (27.322 days) is the time it takes the Moon to do the same, whilst the *sidereal day* (23 hours and 56 seconds) is the time it takes a point on the Earth's surface to rotate once around this same girdle of stars. A large circle on a flattish surface outdoors can readily become your temple under the stars – a sacred place for you to be informed by the sky. *'As above, so below.'* Later, we will see how this can become an accurate calendar and much more.

Summary

The link between astronomy and geometry has been seen to reveal the form and location of stone circles and alignments. In Chapter 4 we will investigate enigmatic stone rings that are not circular at all, discovering that these shapes may be reproduced only with a thorough knowledge of further astronomical observations and precise geometrical techniques.

4

STONE CIRCLES WHICH ARE NOT CIRCULAR

A Geomancy Primer II

Two-thirds of all stone rings are true circles. The remaining third encompass a range of shapes which were repeatedly constructed throughout the entire period of megalith building, each to a precise geometry. These shapes include the ellipse of which there are at least 30 good surviving examples, two main types of flattened circle of which at least 20 good examples exist, two types of stone 'egg-shaped rings' which are rare, but over a dozen may be found on the British mainland, and the exquisite 'compound rings, of which only four good examples are known, one of which is Avebury in Wiltshire, the largest ring of all.

Ellipses

Ellipses are made in exactly the same way as circles, except that there are two centres, called *foci* (Figure 4.1).

EXERCISE 4.1 ELLIPSE CONSTRUCTION

Place two pegs about two MY apart, incorporate both of them within the rope loop and repeat the instructions for the circle in Exercise 3.4 Chapter 3. You will obtain something like Figure 4.1. If you measure the length of the perimeter using the marked rope,

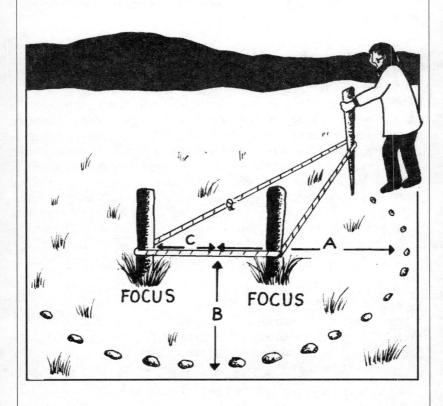

FOCUS

FOCUS

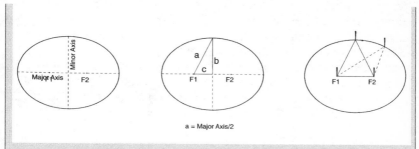

a = Major Axis/2

Figure 4.1 Marking out an ellipse using peg and rope. The single centre of the circle is replaced with two foci. A loop of rope placed around pegs placed at these foci enables the perimeter of an ellipse to be drawn. The geometry is determined from the forming right-angled triangle, *abc*

as if to evaluate *pi*, then what length do you use for the radius? The radius is now variable and ranges between two principal values. The minimum value, *b*, is found when the loop reaches points between and above (or below) the foci. The maximum value, *a*, is found when the loop becomes stretched along the line of the foci. We might suggest that the 'centre' of the ellipse is the point equidistant between the two foci, and the distance from this point to either focus we can term 'c'.

From these values we can totally define the shape of the ellipse. The *minor axis*, becomes 2*b* whilst the *major axis* is 2*a*. The *eccentricity* (departure from circularity and always less than 1) is defined 2*c*/2*a*. The *perimeter* of an ellipse can be measured using a string laid around it or by using special tables to accurately evaluate it. (It is always very close to being (2*a*+2*b*/2). Megalithic folk would probably have used the former method.

An ellipse allows some degree of control over the length of the perimeter and Thom suggested that ellipses were built to obtain integer values for the perimeter (often multiples of 2.5 MY), and as many other main defining features as possible. His evidence, based on meticulous work at over 15 sites, well supports this, although he was not able to discover why ancient folk adopted this design criterium.

There are about 30 surviving ellipses in a state which enables their original geometry to be recovered. As an indication that the builders knew full well what they were doing in laying out ellipses, survey plans will quickly show that several examples were aligned with their major and minor axis coincident with the cardinal points of the compass. Other examples are orientated with the minor axis consistently angled clockwise from north by between 25 and 38 degrees (Figure 4.2). Why, remains a mystery.

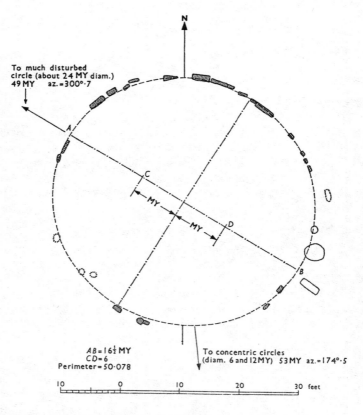

Figure 4.2 Sands of Forvie ellipse (57° 19′.6, 1° 58′.8)

The perimeter of an ellipse can be accurately defined by a right-angled triangle which incorporates *a*, *b* and *c* as its side lengths. Thom showed evidence that the builders were aware of this, and, by measuring the lengths of *a*, *b* and *c* at ellipse sites, he was able to suppose that the builders also wished to make the sides of these triangles integer. As examples, Daviot uses a 12:35:37 'Pythagorean' triangle to define the ellipse, Loanhead of Daviot a 5:13:14, each in MY. Two of the circles at Stanton Drew fit to a 5:12:13 triangle, although the ratio is represented by 15:36:39 at one ellipse and 20:48:52 at the other, also in MY. Interestingly, the major axes lie on the same line.

Whilst it is not yet clear why megalithic architects designed and built ellipses, that they well understood their geometry is clear from the above.

flATTENED CIRCLES

In many books on stone circles, non-circular rings are termed *ovals* or are treated as though their builders failed to obtain a circle and then tolerated a poor design – their implied aim presumably being to build a good circle. This is a total misconception and it contradicts the archaeological theory that the circles were very sacred spaces (and, therefore, worthy of the best efforts of the builders). We shall now discover that these so-called ovals are often 'flattened circles' – a clearly defined design, reproduced all over north-western Europe.

Flattened circles rely on the division of a line into three equal parts – in this case the line becomes the diameter of the finished circle. The simplest way to reproduce the design on the ground is to begin with a *vesica piscis* – two circles whose centres coincide with the circumference of the other. This is a standard geometrical construction (Figure 4.3).

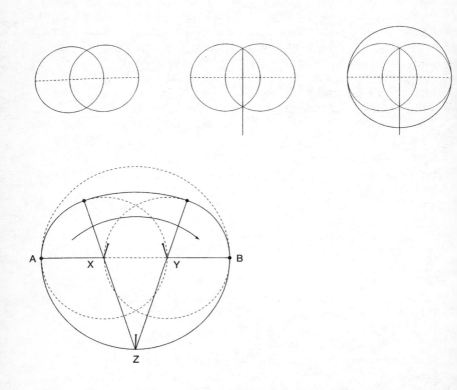

Figure 4.3 Stages in the construction of a Type B flattened circle

EXERCISE 4.1   CONSTRUCTING FLATTENED CIRCLES

Find the centre of the vulva or almond-shaped *vesica* as shown in Figure 4.3 and construct the circumscribing circle as for the circle shape already described. Peg the design as shown and take a rope loop over peg Z and around peg X and to point A on the perimeter of the circle, which is also on the original line. Insert the scribing pen and then simply walk the rope from A to B, whence the required flattening shape will be drawn in the top half of the circle, as long as the rope is allowed to disengage from peg X and then engage with peg Y. The whole sequence is

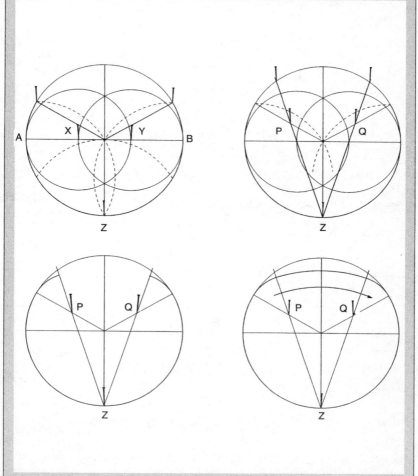

Figure 4.4 Stages in the construction of a Type A flattened circle

itemized in Figure 4.3. This procedure produces Thom's 'Type B' flattened circle.

The 'Type A' flattened circle is slightly different, and my own preferred method of construction enables myself and my student group to construct both types from virtually the same set of procedures (Figure 4.4).

Construct up to the point where pegs X, Y and Z are in place. From peg Z, take a rope loop, of length equal to the radius of the circumscribing circle and mark where it cuts the circumference with another peg. 'Walk' this loop around the perimeter by alternately moving the loop to the new peg and bringing the other end down on to the circumference and pegging it there, as shown in Figure 4.4. You will eventually divide the perimeter into six equal lengths – this being the high-school technique for constructing a hexagon.

From peg Z, extend rope ZX and ZY to points P and Q, and peg these points. The procedure is now just as for the Type B, only pegs P and Q are now used to determine the flattening arcs in the top part of the design.

There are many fine examples of these designs dotted around the United Kingdom and Ireland, two of which are reproduced in (Figure 4.5). Without doubt, the English Lake District is the best area in which to see the finest and largest examples of both types. Why did early man wish to build so many of these shapes? The designs give a different perimeter to 'radius' than for the circle. For the Type A this corresponds to a value of *pi* of 3.058, whilst the Type B suggests *pi* is 2.975. In Chapter 7 the implications of all this will be explored.

STONE EGG-SHAPED RINGS

Stone egg-shaped rings are quite rare, although the two known designs are found from Brittany to Orkney, and the geometry is consistent, again utilizing the right-angled triangle.

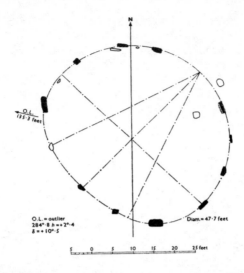

Figure 4.5a Bar Brook (53° 16′6, 1° 34′.9), a large Type B flattened circle in the Derbyshire Peak District

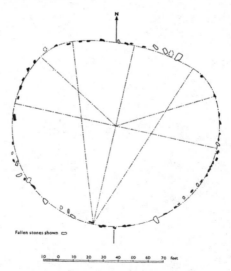

Figure 4.5b Dinnever Hill (50° 35′.4, 4° 38′.8), a large Type A flattened circle in Cornwall

Both designs are produced from two congruent right-angled triangles. In the case of Type I eggs, their adjacent sides are clamped together. For Type II, their hypotenuses are joined. The two designs are shown in Figure 4.6, side by side, for comparison.

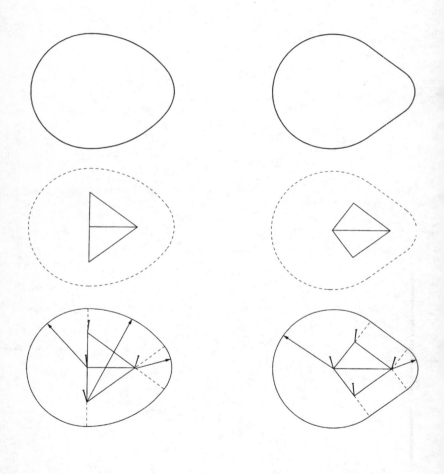

Figure 4.6 The geometry of Type I (left) and Type II (right) egg-shaped rings

Each of the apex points of the triangles are then used to define the arcs of the circles needed to form the final design.

EXERCISE 4.2   CONSTRUCTING EGG-SHAPED RINGS

With some experience of the earlier designs under your belt, you should now be able to mark out and 'rope and peg' good examples of both Type I and Type II eggs. I would recommend using a forming right-angled triangle of 3:4:5, which is the commonest triangle used by the original architects and builders, again measured in integer values of Megalithic yards. Once the triangle is placed out on the ground, the size and shape of the resulting egg's perimeter can be varied infinitely by choosing different dimensions for the radius of the forming semi-circle.

The perimeter of an 'egg' may be calculated relatively easily, either by laying a rope alongside it and then measuring it, or by using the mathematical formulae below:

Type I egg $P = 2\pi r_1 + \pi b - 2aB$, where $\tan B = b/c$
Type II egg $P = 2\pi r_1 + 2c - 2Qb$, where $\tan Q = c/b$

For both these designs, the value of *pi* is larger than 3.14159… because the perimeters are *always* larger than the forming circle. Figure 4.7 shows the plans of some egg-shaped rings.

Recently, amongst the megalithic remains discovered at Nabta, in southern Egypt, lies a perfect Type I egg, some 150 centimetres (60 inches) in diameter, with its entrance marked on the axis of symmetry. Despite its geometry being based exactly on Thom's Type I design, no mention is made of this correspondence in the report, *Megaliths and Neolithic Astronomy in southern Egypt* (from *Nature*, 2/4/98). Using a 'near-Pythagorean' triangle, the Nabta ring shape may be perfectly reproduced. This ring forms part of a complex of sites estimated as being 6,500 years old (Figure 4.11). This is astonishing: an Egyptian stone circle copies exactly the same

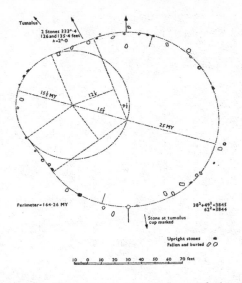

Figure 4.7a Borrowston Rig (55° 46′, 2° 42′), near Edinburgh

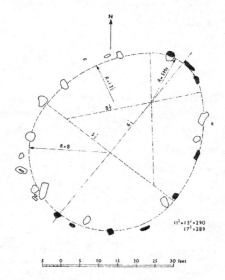

Figure 4.7b Allan Water (55° 20′.8, 2° 50′.1) near Hawick

constructional geometry as circles in the United Kingdom. It was built, allegedly, some *3,000 years earlier*. This small egg takes Thom's work way beyond its European boundaries and our neolithic time frame and poses more questions than it answers.

COMPOUND RINGS

Perhaps the most important of all the stone rings in Britain, the compound rings show a mastery of the techniques already described applied to a much more complex geometrical project. The basic dimensions and perimeters again measure out at multiples of 2.5 MY.

There are only four known survivors of the type, at least whose geometry may be recovered. They are Avebury, in Wiltshire, *Moel ty Uchaf* (Figure 4.8) and Kerry Pole in Powys, Wales, and Easter Delfour in Scotland.

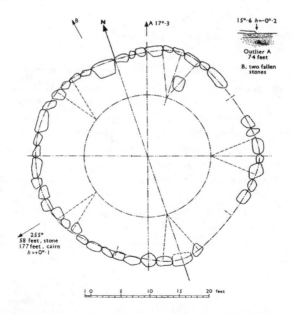

Figure 4.8 Moel ty Uchaf (52° 55'.4, 3° 24'2), near Bala, Wales

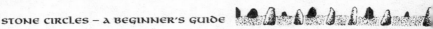

The design for Moel ty Uchaf can be marked out in under two hours, if one knows how to divide a circle into five. But this is a technique not thought to have predated the Greeks – how did megalithic geometers do it? Although Thom refrains from speculation here, as I do, he leaves his readers in no doubt that the rising azimuth of the vitally important fixed star Deneb at this location may have been involved in the construction.

Although spread throughout England, Wales and Scotland, there is a curious similarity of design in the compound rings which cannot be coincidental, and superimposing the plans of Moel ty Uchaf and Kerry Pole inside Avebury (not to scale) demonstrates this. All three sites are essentially pentagonal in shape and all three have the same axis of symmetry as they are also oriented to the compass in the same way. The current theories of archaeology cannot presently account for this complexity of geometry nor the similarities in design (Figures 4.9a and b).

CONCENTRIC RINGS

There are several stone rings which contain a concentric inner circle of stone. Stonehenge is perhaps the best known although the least typical. Two of the most interesting rings are in Scotland, where the geometry of the pentagram and pentagon mark out the design. Miltown even has an outliner stone to confirm the pentagonal intent, whilst Loanhead suggests a decagonal design, with the recumbant entrance stones symmetrically placed within the ten-fold geometry. The diameters of the two rings are 20 MY and 25 MY, with nearby ellipses and circles (not shown) of 6, 10 and 7 MY diameters. Outlier stones indicate and solsticial winter sunrise to extreme accuracy (Figure 4.10).

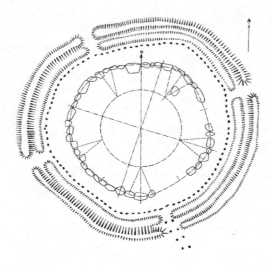

Figure 4.9a Similarity in form. Moel ty Uchaf set inside a plan of Avebury. Both sites are aligned to true north as indicated (not to scale)

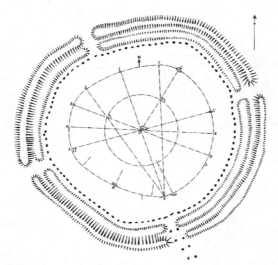

Figure 4.9b Similarity of form between another compound ring (Kerry Pole) and Avebury, both sites aligned with north to the top (not to scale)

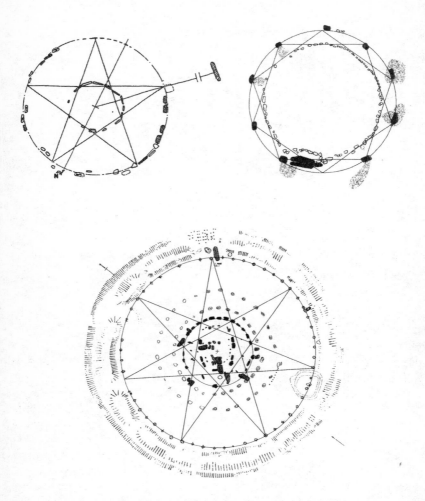

Figure 4.10 Concentric rings: (a) Miltown of Clava (courtesy Anne Macauley) and (b) Loanhead of Daviot (courtesy John Martineau). Pentagonal geometry is clearly shown in the construction of both rings and, at Miltown, even in the outlier stone. (c) The seven-fold connection between the Sarsen Circle and the Aubrey Circle. The inner star 'arms' cross at the mean diameter of the ring of lintels.

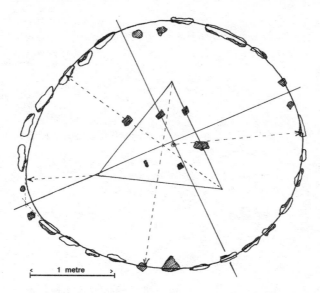

Figure 4.11 The Nabta ring. A Type I egg, built from a Pythagorean triangle.

SUMMARY

Having attempted to replicate some of the actual designs which pepper the wilder parts of the British Isles, you now have to make a rather radical step concerning our ancient past. You do not have to reject one jot of the archaeological evidence concerning the use of circles as ritual and ceremonial places where the dead were revered. You also do not have to reject the chronologies given nor the level of social structure as described within the academic and orthodox textbooks. But you do have to embrace another dimension to the subject which, at present and for many reasons, mainstream culture does not want to face. The reasons for our present culture preferring to remain in denial about matters megalithic have already been discussed.

Either the geometries in this chapter were deliberately applied by megalithic peoples or they were not. If they were deliberate, then a new history of Britain needs writing.

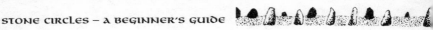

If not, then why are these precise shapes to be found throughout the kingdom and who built them? How was the constructional information transmitted over perhaps 100 generations and spread over 1,500 years and 300,000 square miles?

It is said, wisely, that one ounce of practical experience is worth several pounds of pure theory and speculation. I will leave you with your pegs and ropes, your Megalithic yards and your new-found skill at making 'stone circles' to decide for yourself which model of our past is the more realistic.

5 WHO VISITS STONE CIRCLES?

*O*ver the past ten years, in the course of taking hundreds of people to visit sacred sites, I have identified five clear categories of motives for the visit. You may like to scan over this list and recognize which category or categories stimulate your own interest.

I believe that some understanding of all five categories are needed by the visitor, and it is probably true that if you hold a particularly strong interest in one or perhaps two of the categories below, you will need to study the others if you are to establish a balanced view concerning our megalithic past.

ARCHAEOLOGY

The most traditional of the tools we may use to uncover the past is still a prime discipline by which people learn about stone circles. Although it derives from a pedigree of plunderers, and remains a dreadfully conservative artform, archaeologists provide a most valuable counterbalance against certain factions in other categories, and they are usually very thorough. They ask: What is there? When and how was it placed there and by whom? They will then ask whether the site fits with others and perform the usual academic role of pigeon-holing within categories and/or developing theories and models of the past.

Radio-carbon dating has greatly disturbed the dating systems of archaeology since the Second World War, but the leading exponents have risen superbly to this challenge, whilst others and their textbooks lag decades behind. Public interest in archaeology and the related subject of anthropology is rising: this latter subject is kinder to theories from the other camps listed below.

It remains true, as in John Michell's comment in his book *Megalithomania*, that,

> ... *the most damning criticism of excavations at ancient sites, whether by simple treasure hunters or highly trained archaeologists, is that the sum total of all their labours has contributed scarcely at all to resolving the problem obviously presented by the substantial presence of megalithic monuments, the problem of why they were built.*

Archaeo-astronomy

Also called astro-archaeology, this is a branch of archaeology which studies the astronomical implications of a site. The key rising and setting positions of the Sun, Moon and fixed stars are compared with the geometry of the site and correlations sought. Few archaeologists (or anyone else) understand celestial mechanics nor the complex motions of the Moon, so the casual student need not be surprised that huge errors of common sense are often found in books and articles. To understand megalithic astronomy, you must actually attempt to do some!

Archaeo-astronomers have discovered that site after site takes account of the major risings and settings of the luminaries. The earlier burial chambers and long barrows are often aligned to the rising Sun, whilst John North in his epic book, *Stonehenge*, attempts to show how early humans used star rising and setting positions to determine alignments on the ground at burial chambers and stone circles [*Stonehenge*, HarperCollins (1996). ISBN 0 00 255773 8]

Metrology, sacred geometry and geomancy

Before Alex Thom took his theodolite to over 300 sites, there were few accurate survey plans available for most of the surviving 1,000 or so stone rings in the United Kingdom. The discovery of the unit of length used by the builders, and the design route by which many stone rings were constructed, was first established by Thom in his classic book, *Megalithic Sites in Britain* (Oxford University Press, ISBN 0 19 813148 8), published in 1967. The outcome of his accurate plans and subsequent research has enabled mathematicians and geometers to provide a substantial corpus of evidence that the builders were adepts at certain geometrical techniques which predated by thousands of years the historically enshrined discovery of those same techniques!

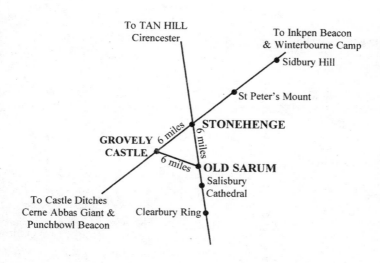

Figure 5.1 Three geometric lines form an equilateral triangle.

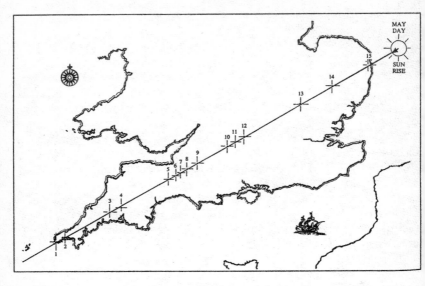

Figure 5.2 The St Michael alignment of sacred sites across southern Britain, which stretches from the furthest western tip of Cornwall to the extreme eastern part of East Anglia: 1. Carn Lês Boel; 2 St. Michael's Mount; 3. Cheesewring; 4. St Michael's Church, Brentor; 5. St Michael's Church, Trull; 6 Burrowbridge Mump; 7. St Michael's Church, Othery; 8. Glastonbury; 9. Stoke St Michael Church; 10. Avebury; 11. Ogbourne St George; 12. St Michael's Church, Clifton Hampden; 13. Royston; 14. Bury St Edmunds; 15. St Margaret's Church, Hopton. (Courtesy of Hamish Miller and Paul Broadhurst)

Professor Keith Critchlow, John Michell, Francis Hitching and Alex Thom were amongst the early pioneers of this aspect of the study of megalithic architecture and design. The geomancy (the accurate measurement, marking out and placement of geometric patterns across a landscape) displayed by some sites remains inexplicably accurate and geometrically superbly elegant. Classic examples in Britain include the famed equilateral triangle formed by Grovely Castle, Stonehenge and Old Sarum, whose sides are exactly 6 miles in length (Figure 5.1); John Michell's 'St Michael' line, which runs

from near Land's End to East Anglia and which aligns to the mayday sunrise (Beltane) connecting tens of ancient sites, many of them megalithic (Figure 5.2). This line is covered in *The Sun and the Serpent* by Hamish Miller and Paul Broadhurst. More recently, the large circular 'leys' around Avebury, proposed by David Furlong in his book, *The Keys to the Temple* (Piatkus, 1997), (page 47) are convincing, and I have discovered a huge triangle which enshrines the secret of the calendar, linking Stonehenge with Lundy, Caldey Island and the Preseli bluestone site (page 98). All of these examples suggest that geomancy was certainly alive and well in ancient Britain, and all of them may be confirmed by anyone with a map and a basic knowledge of trigonometry.

The critical problem now facing researchers in this section is that New Age publishing houses have placed so much indifferent research and so many inaccurate books into the arena that it is difficult for a beginner to separate good material from poor. This is further exacerbated by the fact that academia treats all geomantic work as suspect because it contradicts the order of historical progress, threatening to change the *status quo*. This arena has also always been pervaded by a host of eccentric individualists – amateur mathematicians, numerologists and geometers – working alone within a subject which has no defined boundaries and much faulty data. There is little attempt to collate or regulate any research, although RILKO (Research into Lost Knowledge Organisation) and the American NGCR (National Geocosmic Research) have furnished their readers with a valuable corpus of reliable information.

Leyhunting and dowsing

Leyhunter is a general term for those who visit sites or study locations with a view to showing their linear connection with other sites. The origins of leyhunting may be found elsewhere in this book, and the subject has now become inseparable from 'earth-energies' and 'power-grids'. There is no doubt that ancient sites, from whatever period, do appear to form alignments across the landscape. Many

stone circles are touched tangentially in this way, and it is quite common to find outlying standing stones marking a straight pathway from the site, often independently from any identifiable alignment.

There is enormous room for good research in this category. For years, magazines like *The Leyhunter Journal*, have been challenging the more mindless leyhunter with data and folklore which suggests that 'leys' are ancient ceremonial pathways for the dead taken by the builders of the circles when undertaking their macabre ceremonies. And critics are perfectly in order for reminding leyhunters that the finest of pencil lines ruled across an Ordnance Survey map covers a width of over 30 metres (100 feet)! However, if one applies the criteria listed by Watkins as evidence of a ley, (to wit, that there should be five sites within three or so miles, and these may be fords, gates, stones, stone circles, churches, tumps, mounds, notches in hill-tops, crossroads, holy wells, castles and 'flashes'), then even a newcomer will discover that such sites are apparently not randomly distributed across the map after all, and do exhibit the fascinating property of *linearity*!

Until some genius can define more precisely just what a leyline actually is, and what linearity means, then this category remains perhaps the most subjective of the five as it also attracts amongst its worthy adherents the most colourful range of followers imaginable.

Dowsers have recently been categorized alongside leyhunters. The two subjects can relate, although many dowsers resent the connection. Some archaeologists have used the services of dowsers to establish where to excavate, and to indicate what features exist under the ground, although free admission of such is rarely found in published papers. Dowsers demonstrate that the human physiology is capable of 'knowing' the location of certain substances, such as underground water, ruined buildings or metal. Using pendulums and dowsing rods as 'amplifiers' of this tiny and presumed biological force, they can achieve high success rates at finding objects, trackways and ... yes, even leys. My own research indicates that this category may be where big breakthroughs in understanding the megalithic culture may one day occur.

The 'shamanistic' approach

In recent years, there has been a revival in pagan practice and the concept of shamanism. Shamans undertake spiritual journeys in order to heal the sick, the tribe or the earth, and they claim to contact the spirits of dead ancestors in order to restore the balance of the community. They may use ritual and hallucinogenic drugs in order to obtain the altered state of consciousness they seek. Certain anthropologists are encouraging research into this category if only because it is the one central theme common to all known early tribal cultures, and the work of Jung, Graves, Frazer and Campbell draws heavily on such material.

Many pagans and other folk now visit sacred sites, particularly megalithic sites, in order to honour a solstice, equinox or full moon. This category has, therefore, provided modern folk with the opportunity to reconnect to ritual, and this is no small development. As a reason to visit a stone circle, it probably has at least a 5,000-year-old pedigree or validity. In the past 15 years, thousands of people have begun to re-establish rituals and honour key events in the calendar within the sacred space of stone circles. Neo-pagans have begun to re-enact rituals and ceremonies at site after site and, although some of these are undoubtedly bogus, some are not, and various progressive university anthropology departments (St David's University College, Lampeter and University of East London, London) have hosted conferences and field trips to assess the meaning and function of such a revival.

Within the past five years it is commonplace to discover 'dream-catchers', white quartz, candles, feathers and other shamanistic and ritualistic paraphernalia whenever one visits a stone circle. Whilst some of this is cultural *kitsch*, and some just plain litter, it is indicative of an attempt to reconnect with the fundamental cosmic and elemental truths of life and is, therefore, a form of religious worship. Probably for the first time in nearly 1,000 years, the circles are being used once again for rituals similar to those that archaeologists suggest were in use 5,000 years ago. If this arouses

complaint and fear amongst those who feel that the sites are being defiled it scarcely lessens the social importance of the rekindling of ritual within the circles. And if some of the 'worshippers' are riding on contemporary fashion, and/or fail to understand in the slightest what these rituals mean, many churchgoers also fall within the same category of ignorance and compliance with social fashion and no one seems to bat an eyelid. In this context, it is worth observing that many of Britain's churches are emptying, with an ageing congregation, whilst the circles are filling with younger people attempting to connect with the forces of evolution. Both churches and stone circles are ultimately temples dedicated to these forces.

These, then, are five categories which form the main reasons for visiting stone circles. There is certainly a sixth, for folk often go to circles simply because they are excellent places just to hang out, or ponder the meaning of life. Henry James put this very well,

> There is something in Stonehenge almost reassuring; and if you are disposed to feel that life is rather a superficial matter, and that we soon get to the bottom of things, the immemorial grey pillars may serve to remind you of the enormous backdrop of time.

Whatever your reasons for visiting these sites, you are connecting in some measure with 'The Ancestors' and with the cosmic forces of evolution. What that means is probably different for each and every visitor.

6

UNDERSTANDING MEGALITHIC ASTRONOMY

A stronomy is not taught in any depth within our school curriculum and there is widespread ignorance amongst today's 'educated' folk concerning even the basic motions of the Sun, Moon and stars. This situation is made worse by the insistence on heliocentric (Sun-centred) models of the cosmos. The circle builders performed geocentric (Earth-centred) astronomy and, using their surviving remnants, a 12 year old may readily forecast the date of the next eclipse.

Our ancestors would have recognized more of the significance of the Sun and Moon to human life than we do today. The seasonal changes caused by the Sun's annual climb, higher and higher, each day into the warming sky to midsummer, followed by its retreat lower in the sky each day to midwinter cold and long nights was not then masked by our central heating and artificial lighting. The Sun's rising and setting points on the horizon moving daily northward at the approach of spring and summer and similarly southward at the approach of autumn and winter are obvious if one lives outdoors. The range of sunrises and sunsets is shown in Figure 6.1

Daily contact with the Moon's changing phases and her constant and rapidly nightly motion anticlockwise against the stars, led to the need to understand more about the *White Queen* who claws the tides up and down twice daily. Her monthly rhythm synchronizes both to the tidal changes and to the menstrual cycle and, therefore, to human fertility. Longer-term rhythms of the Moon reveal the cycles of eclipse types and perhaps something else.

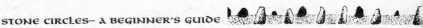

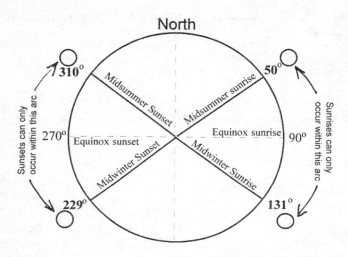

Figure 6.1 The range of sunrises and sunsets at the latitude of Stonehenge

The Dance of the Sun and Moon

The Moon begins her monthly phases as a sliver of silver on the *left-hand side* of the Sun. She is then mainly an object of the daytime skies and appears only briefly after the Sun has set. Each successive night after that, she becomes more and more a *'Lady of the Night'* as the waxing phases increase the crescent to a quarter and then a full moon, taking about 13 days to complete. Only at full moon does she 'escape' the Sun, becoming completely nocturnal, lighting up the whole night sky and enabling humans and animals to see during the night. Thereafter, the waning cycle progressively diminishes the light as the Moon sets later and later in the morning skies until, again after about 13 days, she may be glimpsed only as a tiny crescent on the *right* of the Sun. The Moon then disappears for about three days, lost in the glare of the Sun at the new moon. This complete *lunation cycle* takes 29.53059 days (Figure 6.2).

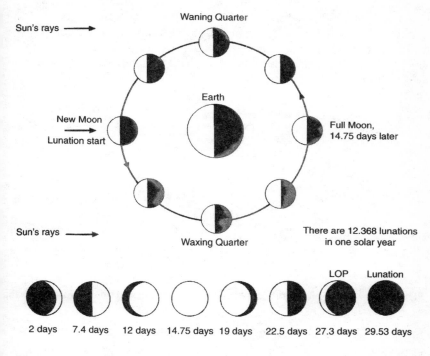

Figure 6.2 The lunation cycle of 29½ days. The standard, although incorrect, lunation diagram beloved of school textbooks, showing lunar phases. The sidereal lunar orbital period (marked LOP) takes 27.322 days to complete and is independent of the phase of the Moon

If you observe the Moon on a regular basis, you cannot fail but note that each night finds the Moon moved 13 degrees against the fixed stars from the position held the previous night. It is useful to make this observation, even estimate the angle by pointing the right arm towards the stars where the Moon was passing yesterday, and the left arm to where she resides today. A protractor is more accurate!

Once this vital measurement is taken, then it soon becomes evident that it takes the Moon slightly less than 28 days to return to the

same part of the sky. This is the sidereal lunar month of 27.322 days, and is independent of the Sun, unlike the lunation cycle. Figure 6.3 makes it clear the distinction between these two 'monthly' cycles of the Moon. There are just over 12 lunation cycles in a year, and 13 sidereal months, and we shall meet these numbers again when discussing legend and the calendar.

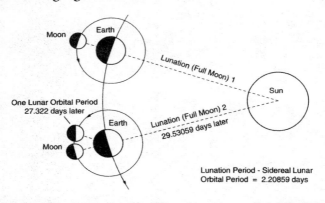

Figure 6.3 Why the lunar orbital period and lunation period differ. (Not to scale)

Each month, the Moon more or less copies the entire annual range of rises and sets undertaken by the Sun in a year. Always at her most northerly risings and settings each month when passing through the stars of the constellation of Gemini, she then rises highest in the sky. The most southerly risings occur when transiting the constellation of Sagittarius, when she may barely rise above the horizon in northerly latitudes. (In the *tropical* zodiac signs these remain Cancer and Capricorn, as does our Tropic of Cancer and Capricorn – neither are affected by the precessional cycle which moves the actual constellations around the seasons, taking 26,000 years to complete the process. Currently, the two cycles are 26 degrees 'out of sync', the Sun may be found rising at 5° of the constellation Pisces at the vernal equinox.)

The full moon is therefore brightest and highest at midwinter – the Sun is then in the constellation of Sagittarius and the full moon must thus be opposite this, in the constellation Gemini (and sign

Cancer, its ruling sign). Now the full moon rises and sets like the Sun at midsummer. *In other words, the full moon always behaves opposite to the Sun.* Most people know that the Sun fails to rise high in the sky during winter and rises very high in summer. The full moon reverses this, rising highest in winter and lowest in summer.

The breath of the Moon

Regular observation over some years will establish that the Moon's extreme rising and setting positions 'breathe' in and out either side of those of the Sun, taking 18.62 years to complete a cycle. Over 230 lunations, the Moon will be seen rising well to the north of the Sun's midsummer rising and setting positions and well to the south of the midwinter positions. This is the *major standstill*; 9.3 years later the Moon's extreme rising and setting positions each month will fall by an equal amount inboard of those of the Sun's annual cycle – this is the *minor standstill*. I call the effect the *lunstices* (Figure 6.4).

The variation in major and minor standstill azimuths depends on the latitude of the location. In southern Britain the major and minor

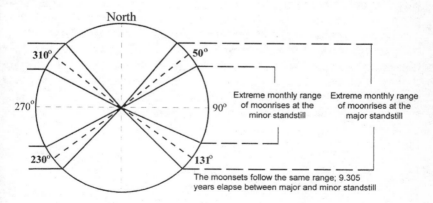

Figure 6.4 The variation in extreme monthly moonrises and sets (at the latitude of Stonehenge) over the 18.618-year 'lunstice' cycle of the lunar nodes. The total angular change is twice 5.14/cos (latitude of site)

standstill positions are both placed about 10 degrees from the solstice positions of the Sun. Thus, at each site, a researcher looking for astronomical alignments needs to know the extreme solstice positions and the extreme lunar rising and setting positions. A computer program will assist here, *Skyglobe* being useful for understanding these rhythms of the sky whilst sitting in the comfort of your own home. Table 6.1 gives approximate values.

Because the tilt in the Earth's axis has reduced by nearly half a degree since 3000 BCE, these extreme rising and setting angles of the Sun and Moon have narrowed since the circles were built. Luckily, calculators and computers can account for this change and locate where on the horizon all these things occurred when the circle was built. This is beyond the scope of this book, but a program in BASIC is included to assist the more adventurous reader (see Appendix).

The numbers of the Sun and Moon

Any attempt to tally the numbers of Sun and Moon cycles will lead the modern reader into a useful place where much myth and legend can be better understood. It can also help a student to understand the inevitable choices and compromises which must be made in designing any calendar. I believe it can also explain the purpose of certain sites. Our circle builders were *numerate* if not literate, and their constructions confirm that they positively wallowed in numerical relationships, ratios and proportions relating to soli-lunar astronomy.

One useful starting place for the following exercise is to ask after how long will the Sun and Moon take to return to the same positions in the sky after a given whole number of years has elapsed? This yields the table here (Table 6.2), and immediately suggests the design route for Avebury, where inner circles of 27 and 29 stones strongly support their use as recorders of both lunar

Table 6.1 Maximum and minimum sunrise and sunset azimuths, with 18.62-year lunar cycle variance from solar azimuths

Latitude of site (degrees)	Lunar angle + and − (degrees)	Summer solstice (SS) R = rise, S = set (azimuth °)		Winter solstice (WS) R = rise, S = set (azimuth °)	
		SSSR	SSSS	WSSR	WSSS
30 Giza	5.93	62.05	297.94	117.89	242.11
40 Greece	6.71	58.01	302.00	121.92	238.08
45 Bordeaux	7.27	54.97	305.02	124.95	235.08
48 Carnac	7.68	52.66	307.34	127.25	232.74
50 Cornwall	8.00	50.85	309.15	129.06	230.94
51 Stonehenge	8.17	49.84	310.15	130.06	229.94
52 Rollrights	8.35	48.76	311.23	131.14	228.86
53 Derby	8.54	47.60	312.40	132.30	227.70
54 Lancaster	8.74	46.34	313.66	133.56	226.44
55 Carlisle	8.96	44.97	315.03	134.93	225.07
56 Edinburgh	9.19	43.47	316.53	136.41	223.58
57 Aberdeen	9.44	41.83	318.17	138.05	221.95
58 Ullapool	9.70	40.02	319.98	139.85	220.15
59 Orkneys	9.98	38.00	321.99	141.85	218.14
60 Lerwick	10.28	35.74	324.25	144.10	215.89

To obtain the Major and Minor standstill azimuths of the Moon for a given latitude, add and subtract the 'Lunar angle' given, to the extreme solar azimuths.

The assumed axial tilt angle is 23.93°, about the value in 2500 BCE. The table assumes a zero altitude horizon.

cycles, whilst the outer circle of 99 stones (107 stones if we include the aligned entrance stones to the West Kennett Avenue) serves admirably as a recorder of the eight-year soli-lunar cycle (Figure 6.5). Venus also follows an eight-year cycle, which may have been connected with Avebury (see later in this chapter for details on Venus), and the Cretan myth of the Minotaur supports the importance of the eight-year cycle in ancient times.

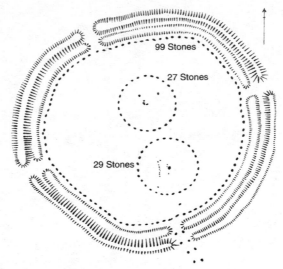

99 Stones

27 Stones

29 Stones

Figure 6.5 The layout of the Avebury circles (see text for calendrical instructions)

The use of 19 stones at many sites, including Stonehenge, suggests that the designers understood the Metonic cycle, when, after precisely 19 years have elapsed, 235 lunations have also elapsed (to within 2 hours), leaving the Sun and Moon in the same relative positions they held exactly 19 years previously, on the same date and more or less the same time of day. The historian Diodorus' accounts of Britain included knowledge of a temple dedicated to Apollo where the stars revisited the site 'every nineteen years'. One may conclude that this refers to Stonehenge and its connection with the Metonic cycle – the outer bluestone ring contains 19 stones.

EXERCISE 6.1

How many (i) outer stones, and (ii) entrance stones, would Avebury have needed if one wished to record the 19-year cycle above? What is the difference between the two? Repeat for the actual Avebury stones and comment on your answer.

Table 6.2 Sun and Moon repeat cycles

Years	Days	Lunations	Sid. months	Misalignment	
3	1095.73	37.105	40.104	–3.09 days	
8	2921.94	98.95	106.94	+1.477 days	Avebury – see text?
					(8 years Venus cycle)
19	6939.60	**235**	253	2.08 hrs	**Metonic Cycle**

[= (2×8) +3] – the misalignments above for 8 and 3 years almost cancel out.

Other interesting soli-lunar patterns

5	1826.211	61.84 (100 × φ)	66.84	+4.68 days	Coligny calendar?

Solar 'repeat rising' cycles

4	1460.96	(49.47)	(53.47)	–45 minutes	365+365+365+366
					(leap year day)
33*	12052.99	(408.15)	(441.15)	**–10.70 minutes**	**Perfect solar return**

* The 33-year cycle brings an exact repeat rising from behind a horizon marker (stone). It is the number found throughout 'solar-hero' or 'divine hero' myths of Celtic mythology and its connection with the crucifixion and resurrection of Jesus, at 33 years of age, is evident. The Mayan *Dresden Codex*, an eclipse table, is also of this duration, terminating after 405 lunations – the last eclipse possible in the 33-year cycle.

The solar tropical year is 365.242199 days in length; average lunation period is 29.53059 days; sidereal lunar month 27.322 days.

Eclıpses

Solar eclipses occur when a new moon finds the Sun, Moon and Earth exactly in alignment, a rare event indeed at the latitude of the British Isles, as the excitement over the 'Cornish Eclipse' of 11 August 1999 demonstrates. Lunar eclipses occur at a full moon when the alignment becomes Sun, Earth and Moon. These are commonplace and are seen by the entire night half of the planet – thus there is a 50 per cent chance of seeing every lunar eclipse – and they average three to four over two years.

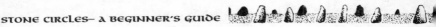

Solar and lunar eclipses do not occur each month because the Moon's orbit is slewed at just over 5° to the Sun's apparent orbit around the zodiac (the *ecliptic*); the orbits intersect at only two places. So, although every 14 days the Moon crosses this intersection, at points directly opposite each other, *only* if the Sun is currently passing near to either one of these two crossing points – called the lunar *nodes* – will an eclipse take place. This happens every 173 days and is called an *eclipse season*. The *eclipse year* is twice this, at 346 days long.

There is one more complication – the nodal points rotate backwards around the calendar, synchronized to the 18.62-year cycle of the Moon's risings and settings. We know that ancient astronomers were observing this cycle and making alignments to mark it. They would have naturally come to understand that where eclipses took place in the calendar was linked to this cycle; noticing that, each year, eclipses occur an average 19 days earlier in the calendar. It should, therefore, be no surprise that a device to accurately predict eclipses appears to have been fabricated by megalithic culture.

The Aubrey calendar and eclipse predictor of Stonehenge is an elegant and minimal design to enable the prediction of eclipses to the nearest day. Like Avebury, it remains in good enough condition to still work perfectly, after 5,000 years (Figure 6.6).

Twenty-eight markers define the best possible accuracy for a Sun, Moon analogue model using a minimum number of markers. However, twice 28 is coincidentally thrice 18.61, enabling the simple 56-marker model illustrated in Figure 6.6 to predict eclipses, in addition to informing the user about lunar position and phase, the calendar date and, indeed, all the requirements listed in *Saltair na Rann* (page 15) as required knowledge for educated people.

Stonehenge and the earlier Avebury, in their numbers alone, support a belief in a highly sophisticated astronomical understanding, centred in Wessex before 3000 BCE. It is the very earliest phase of Stonehenge which contains the soli-lunar calendar and eclipse predictor.

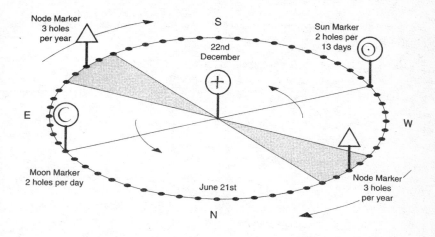

Figure 6.6 The Stonehenge Calendar adapted for Eclipse Prediction. The two node markers define two eclipse zones (shaded) in the year when full or new moons will produce an eclipse. They are moved clockwise one hole three times a year. The full moon shown above (20 October) would *not* produce an eclipse – it lies outside of the eclipse zone. The eclipse zones rotate backwards around the calendar over an 18.6-year cycle.

The stars

Rising and setting stars do so at the same angles every day, although over the centuries this, too, changes. At midwinter, if one wants to know the time during the long cold nights, the sequence of setting of Altair (8 p.m.), Vega (10 p.m.) and Deneb (midnight) followed by Arcturus rising (1 a.m.), Sirius setting (4 a.m.) and Procyon setting (7 a.m.) forms a useful stellar 'clock'. Due to precession and axial tilt changes, the azimuth positions of rise and set of the stars, together with the times of rise and set, inform us that our megalithic

forebears would have timed their night sky differently. Again, computer programs can account for this, and professor John North has produced in *Stonehenge* (page 12) a useful star map for the year 3000 BCE.

A further set of complications present themselves to amateur circle visitors who wish to understand the astronomy of a site. The local horizon will normally not have zero altitude unless looking out over the sea from the beach. All the azimuths will depend on the altitude angle of the horizon, particularly for stars which are nearly circumpolar, such as Deneb.

The second complication is that stars cannot be seen rising or setting to or from a level horizon – they disappear a degree or so from their rising and setting positions. This angle is called the *extinction angle* and combines with atmospheric distortion to worsen the accuracy of measurements of stellar azimuths. Some sites, like Castle Rigg, used high-altitude horizons (called 'mountains') to neatly avoid both distortions.

Whatever, the amateur can use current software and common sense to recognize the useful limits of what can be achieved to recover possible alignments to stellar risings and settings at stone circles. It certainly cannot be undertaken with just a hand-held compass, although such equipment may, with intelligence, usefully signal an initial clue.

The planets

There is no concrete evidence to indicate that ancient megalithic astronomers were aligning their circles to the visible planets. It must be the case that they would have been fascinated by their cycles and obvious changes in size, prominence and direction of motion against the fixed stars. Because the planets stray a little from the ecliptic, it would be difficult to understand why their rise and set positions would be useful to megalithic folk; perhaps their numerology and geometry would have been of more interest.

For example, the planet Venus traces out a near-perfect pentagram in its *synodic* cycle as seen from the Earth, taking eight years almost to the day to complete the five 'star-arms'. Thus, in our dim past, Venus was linked with the number five and Friday remains our fifth day of the week (Vendredi) – both Frigga and Venus were love goddesses of ancient mythology. The three annual retrograde 'loops' of Mercury link that planet to the number three, preserved in our third day of the week being named after Mercury (Wodensday, Mercredi). It is well worth studying the planet's cycles and linking the resulting numbers with mythology and legend. In Chapter 7, we will apply this to the numbers of the Sun and Moon.

Summary

The circles were built to observe a rather different sky than that which we can observe today. This means that a circle may be dated if one knows the intended alignments. It also informs us that some of these artefacts are badly out of date, like last year's calendar. Perhaps it is high time we encouraged the building of some new circles which are temples under, and dedicated to, the cosmos we actually experience today. Meanwhile, because the cycles of the Sun and Moon remain much as they were, the existing temples at Stonehenge and Avebury still 'work', and could be restored to perform their original implied task of monitoring soli-lunar cycles. Perhaps you could write to English Heritage.

7

THE RE-EMERGENCE OF MEGALITHIC SCIENCE

*I*t *is important to include within these pages some of the important aspects of stone circles which presently occupy no space within the orthodox view of megalithic culture. Amongst these aspects is the role of legend and myth in preserving the megalithic secrets, and the structure of the calendar with its relationships to the motions of the Sun and Moon.*

THE MEGALITHIC LEGACY AS CALENDRAIC ARTEFACTS

The obvious use of stone circles as sites aligned to key points in the calendar leads naturally into a study of how the calendar originated. In this, we have some spectacular examples from the megalith builders. The degree of flattening created by both the Type A and Type B flattened circles allows an easy extraction of the lunar year (354.367 days) and the eclipse year (346.62 days) respectively. If the defining circle perimeter is taken to represent the solar year of 365.242 days, then the perimeter of the flattened circle becomes the eclipse year (Type B) or the lunar year (Type A). The compound ring, *Moel ty Uchaf*, also yields the lunar year in the same fashion. These may be coincidences, but beyond the scope of this book lies another astronomical mystery connected with both types of flattened circle which suggests otherwise. There are still huge sections of the megalithic puzzle to be solved!

The Aubrey circle, Stonehenge's soli-lunar calendar *par excellence*, is a supremely elegant (and minimal) design for capturing the motions of both the Sun and the Moon on to the Earth, in order to understand the calendar (see Figure 6.6). By actually using the design, it quickly becomes apparent that it instantly shows the solar position (i.e. the date and the season), the lunar position (the Moon's position against the stars) and the lunar phase. Although this is all the calendar maker usually wants to know, the same model will also show when eclipses may be expected, the state of the sea tides and which stars will be visible in the current night sky.

The numbers of the evolutionary engine

This model relies on some numerical facts. First, there is a reciprocity between the Sun and the Moon. The Moon moves about 13 degrees per day (Figure 7.1), taking approximately 28 days to complete a circuit of the skies, whilst the Sun moves 1 degree per day, *one thirteenth* of the rate of the Moon, and therefore takes approximately 13 × 28 days (364 days) to complete a circuit.

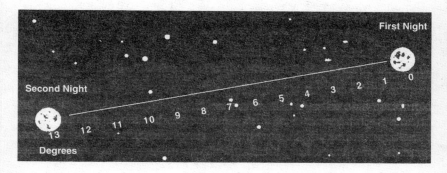

Figure 7.1 The Moon's daily motion against the stars. Every 24-hour period, the Moon moves an average of 13.176 degrees along the ecliptic. In just over one hour the Moon has moved by its own diameter against the fixed stars

The year naturally falls into four phases – those we call spring, summer, autumn and winter and which are defined by the two equinoxes and two solstices. The number 28 divides by four. The month also naturally divides into four periods of *seven* days – waxing quarter, full moon, waning quarter and new moon. The Moon orbits the Earth 13 times a year. The factors which these immutable facts reveal are 4, 7 and 13, which multiplied together also give 364 – a remarkable close figure (99.72 per cent) to the actual year, and one which also conveniently divides by four.

Children at school are taught that there are seven days in a week, four weeks in a month and twelve months in a year. Which is fine until one bright ten year old multiplies these out and gets 336 for the length of the year! If she's really bright, her suggestion that there's a lunar month missing (336 + 29 = 365) will provoke the whole class into a meaningful discussion as to what exactly went wrong with the calendar and why don't we have a 13-month year? Why indeed?

The irrational calendar

Our present calendar, based on 365 days, produces irrational numbers whenever one attempts to do anything real with it. It only divides by *five* (has anyone heard of Vivaldi's *Five Seasons*?), gives 52.142857… weeks in the year, 30.41666 days to a 'month' wholly unrelated to the Moon, and all the festival dates fall on a different day of the week every year. It divides neither by four, seven nor twelve, whilst the 364-day calendar offers nothing but whole number divisions for actual events: 52 weeks in a year, 7 days in a week, a 28-day month (lying between the two lunar periods) and all the festival days occur on the same day of the week year after year. The *only* change from the hapless calendar we struggle with today is that a leap-year day must be added *every year* instead of every four years, and *two* days every *fourth year*. And there must be 13 months. Any bright ten year old can see which is the more sensible calendar. Why cannot we change it and why is the number 13 so unlucky?

Thirteen months versus twelve months

At this point we enter the world of myth, which parallels the numerical conflicts inherent in the biggest dilemma facing calendar makers. Is the 'month' to be taken as the time it takes for the Moon to complete a circuit in the heavens (the sidereal month, of which there are just over 13 a year) or do we prefer the *lunation cycle* (the Moon's phases – of which there are just over 12 a year)? The megalithic astronomers needed to know *both* in order to understand the skies. Is this why Avebury contains circles of 27 and 29 stones adjacent to each other, and why these same numbers may be found at other multiple circle sites such as *The Hurlers* in Cornwall?

The most ancient written texts, in the *Rig Veda*, inform us that 'it is the Moon which shapes the year'. The choice of 12 or 13 months is not to be taken lightly, it seems, and our Western culture has adopted 12 months as the 'rational' choice, leading to our most unholy irrational calendar. The folly of this choice also shouts out to us from our myths, fairy stories and legends, because it is misaligned to the natural evolutionary forces.

The megalithic legacy as folklore and legend (solar heroes and sleeping beauties)

Throughout the world may be found the same legends. A hero figure emerges from obscurity to become a king or saviour. He then recruits 12 disciples, knights or soldiers to assist in this mission, thus becoming the thirteenth member of the group, and is eventually killed or sacrificed, thereby immortalized. The story is the same, even in many of the lesser details, and its heroes include Jesus, King Arthur and the Mexican Kukulcan. Always, the numbers are 12 and 13,

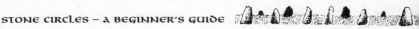

with the thirteenth offering salvation, redemption and completeness. With Arthur, we even get a Round Table.

The fairy story of *Sleeping Beauty*, sometimes called *Briar Rose*, is essentially conveying a similar message. A king and a queen desire a child. Eventually, the queen is able to conceive and gives birth to a remarkably beautiful girl-child. The king wishes to invite all the wise women to a feast in order that they can confer a blessing each on the princess. There are 13 wise women in the land but, alas, the king has only 12 golden plates. Inevitably, the thirteenth wise woman is left out from the invitation list and, equally inevitably, she bursts in on the proceedings and places a curse on both the kingdom and the child, both of which eventually succumb on the child's thirteenth (and in some versions her fourteenth or fifteenth) birthday. The kingdom then falls asleep, awaiting the handsome prince who can hack his way through all the briars and brambles in order to kiss the princess and restore the kingdom once again, and bring about the 'happy ever after' ending.

No one complains about their fate in this charming story. Leaving out the thirteenth wise woman *naturally* invokes the curse. It is an inevitable consequence of excluding the feminine, lunar aspects of life. The kingdom then falls asleep until the beauty of the princess – the 'feminine' component – is once again accepted and valued. The meaning of the 12 golden plates will now be understood by the reader, as will the other symbols within these stories.

Sexing the Stones

The solar hero myths of the Celtic world and elsewhere are truly connected, through their numbers, with the Sun and its cycles. In our mythology and legends the Sun is considered masculine whilst the Moon is considered feminine. It is of interest that the solar cults of the world represent the Sun through lines and rectangles in their art, whilst curves and circles are taken to represent the Moon. This practice is hinted at within many stone circles and avenues, where alternate square and rounded stones may be found. Avebury,

Stonehenge and the Hurlers are amongst the best sites to view this deliberate use of two quite distinct shapes, although we do not know for certain why the builders incorporated such a distinction (Figure 7.2).

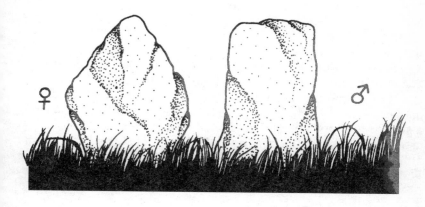

Figure 7.2 Examples of female (left) and male (right) stones, as found at megalithic sites (here, The Hurlers, Cornwall)

The silver fraction

The reality of the 12/13 dilemma is that the actual number of full moons in the year falls between these two numbers, at 12.368. The over-run, 0.368, which is almost exactly 7/19 as a fraction, is the single most important number needed by a calendar designer. It represents the difference between the lunar year of 354 days and the solar year of 365 days. Without knowledge of this fraction – *the silver fraction of the Moon*, there can be no accurate calendar, no eclipse prediction and no grasp of the celestial mechanics of the Sun and Moon. (For eclipse prediction, you will also need to know the length of the *eclipse year*, 346.6 days.)

It inevitably follows that a culture actively researching the skies and attempting to understand the motions of the Sun and Moon would

eventually discover and then use this fraction within their calendars. We would expect to find the silver fraction (0.368 of a lunation or 10.875 days) incorporated within artefacts, myth and legend from the megalithic period, and this is, in fact, the case. The reciprocal of 0.368 is 2.72, which immediately alerts us to something odd, as 2.72 is the length of the Megalithic yard in feet. Putting aside why we should be measuring lengths in feet for a moment, we discover from this numerical fact that if we let the Megalithic yard (2.72 feet) represent one lunation, then 0.368 lunation (the silver fraction) becomes *exactly* one foot. We are then also confronted with the strange fact that the remaining 0.632 MY, which is 1.72 feet just happens to be the length of the Egyptian Royal Cubit, and we enter a strange territory indeed. These relationships, which connect astronomy with *mensuration*, a word whose root stems from 'moon' although few seem to know why anymore, are shown in Table 7.1. Perhaps we should refer to our national temple at this point.

Table 7.1 The relationship between megalithic units of length and astronomic constants

A European unit	**The Megalithic yard – 2.72 feet in length**	
	can be made up from	
An Egyptian unit		
One Royal cubit – 20.63 inches	plus	**one foot – 12 inches**
		A Sumerian unit
1.72 ft + 1 ft = 2.72 ft = 1 MY		
1 Royal cubit + 1 foot = 1 MY		
– The Astronomical Realities –		
One lunation (29.53059 days)		
	equals	
One lunar node 'day' (18.618 days)		**plus the lunar over-run**
		(10.875 days) or 0.368 of a lunation

One foot = 0.368 Megalithic yards and one year = 12.368 lunations, therefore the lunar over-run is the difference between the solar year of 365.242199 days and the lunar year of 354.36708 days. The Megalithic yard represents a lunation period.

At Stonehenge we find that the outer diameter of the Sarsen circle compared to that of the Aubrey circle yields the silver fraction. Once one understands that this key calendrical ratio links feet to Megalithic yards, then it becomes laughably obvious that this will be the case – for the outer Sarsen diameter is 104 feet, whilst the Aubrey diameter is 104 MY.

At Stonehenge we also find the numbers 12 and 13 are repeated as lengths to 0.25 per cent accuracy at two important places. The longer side of the station stone rectangle and its diagonal – also the diameter of the Aubrey circle – relate by the ratio 12:13. From the centre of Stonehenge to the heelstone forms a ratio of 12:13 with the Aubrey diameter. Each 'unit' is exactly 8 MY in length.

The Lunation Triangle

At this point we can combine geometry and astronomy to reveal a most useful artefact. The station stone rectangle contains, with its diagonal, a 5:12:13 Pythagorean triangle. In between the 12 and 13 sides of this triangle it is possible to draw a new hypotenuse whose length is exactly the number of lunations (full moons) in the year – 12.368. That this divides the '5' side exactly into the ratio 3:2 should cause a *frisson* of excitement because it is true that, using only a knotted cord of 31 equally spaced knots, it is possible to peg out a geometrical shape which can deliver within minutes the vital silver fraction of the Moon, to 0.008 per cent accuracy.

EXERCISE 7.1

Using Pythagoras' theorem, prove the last paragraph mathematically, ($12.368^2 = 12^2 + 3^2$). What is the value of 12.368^2? Does this appear at all curious?

EXERCISE 7.2

Using the knotted rope, peg out a 5:12:13 triangle. The right angle is produced automatically whenever one pegs the '12' side of the triangle and brings the '5' and '13' sides together. Bring the '13' side down to the 3:2 point on the '5' side – it cuts this point having length 12.368 inside the triangle. Confirm the length of the *silver fraction* and also the length of rope which falls outside the triangle.

At this point the calendar may be completely defined. The 12.368 length can now be proportioned on to the 'year' rope, which can be either the '12' or original '13' side of the triangle. The full and new moons can readily be dated for the year to come. If the Megalithic yard is chosen for the equally spaced lengths on the rope, then the 12.368 length is 12 MY plus *one foot*. To mark the dates of the full moons *one inch* must be *subtracted* progressively from each of the 12 equal lengths of the '12' side of the triangle (one inch for the first month, two inches for the second and so on). This assumes a 12-month year with the '12' side of the triangle representing 365.242 days.

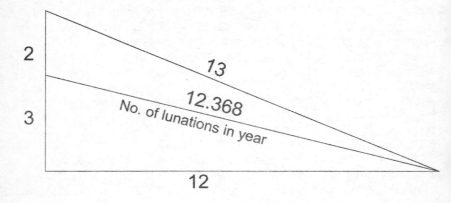

Figure 7.3 The lunation triangle

I have called this remarkable construction the *lunation triangle* (Figure 7.3). It ties up known megalithic astronomic intentions, their fascination with geometry and their unit of length. It also suggests the foot as the *original* unit of length. Why? Could it be that the foot is one-thousandth part of a degree of arc along the Earth's equatorial circumference, acceptance of which places a new dimension on the culture which built the megaliths – primarily, knowledge that the Earth is round and had been accurately measured before 3000 BCE?

BIBLICAL AND GEOMANTIC
MESSAGES FROM THE PAST

An entirely ample description of the lunation triangle may be found in the last chapter of St John's Gospel, in the Bible. Here, Christ, as the thirteenth member of the 12 disciples, meets them for the third time since his resurrection, on the shoreline adjacent to where a number of disciples have been fishing from boats, to no avail. Three disciples are named, two are not. Jesus suggests to them that they cast their nets on the 'right side' of the boat. They then catch 153 fishes in the net. Now, go back and repeat exercise 7.1, if you wish to discover the esoteric meaning of this oldest fishing yarn.

A rather large lunation triangle may be discovered veering westwards from Stonehenge, taking in Lundy Island, Caldey Island and the Preseli bluestone site as the points on the short '5' side (Figure 7.4). Lundy lies *exactly* west of Stonehenge. Lundy, Caldey and the bluestone site are spaced to a ratio of 3:2 and lie exactly on a north–south line, each is intervisible from the other two. The old Welsh name for Lundy, *Ynys Elen*, means 'the island of the elbow or angle'. Strange material!

This north–south line continues southwards to embrace two sites connected with the Arthurian legends – his conception place at Tintagel and Castle Dore where the story of Tristram and Iseulte originated. The ratio between these sites and Lundy is also 3:2. Glastonbury, where Arthur is allegedly buried and where Christianity

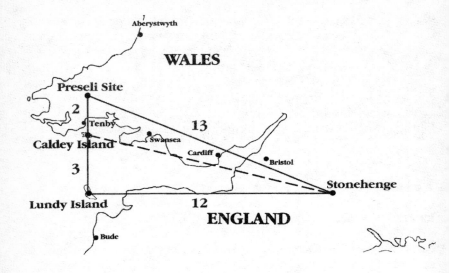

Figure 7.4 The Stonehenge–Preseli lunation triangle

is supposed to have begun in Britain, lies on the '12' side of the triangle, as does Dunster, where Arthur is supposed to have spent his childhood. It is also useful to follow this north–south line northwards – 4° 41′ West – past Cardigan Island, Bardsey Island and the Isle of Man. Important ancient Celtic sites lie on or very close to each of these places, suggesting to this writer that the Celtic monks knew of the megalithic legacy left in Britain and grafted the Arthurian and other legends on to it. I suggest that the Christ story and that of Arthur share the same mythic roots.

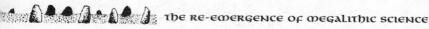

Summary

The material in this chapter should awaken the reader to some of the larger cultural implications which emerge from a *holistic* study of stone circles. When myth, geometry, astronomy and mathematics interlock sensibly, we can glimpse the megalithic science and the philosophy which lay behind so much laborious work all those centuries ago. This science and this philosophy are seen as fully fledged right at the outset of the megalithic period, suggesting the existence of a high culture prior to 3500 BCE.

We are fortunate that sufficient sites have survived to allow us to appreciate their astonishing message. Similarly, we can marvel at the tenacity of ancient myths and legends, whose tales, however unlikely, support the same numbers, astronomy and geometry we can find at the monuments. You are now recommended to read some of the books in Further Reading and to visit some of the sites upon which this guide is based (Appendix).

appendix

The top twenty UK sites to visit

The list below covers 20 of the best sites to visit and covers the whole of the United Kingdom. It is possible to visit more than one in the area during your visit. There is never more than 70 miles to travel to see one of these sites.

For a complete guide, refer to *A Guide to the Stone Circles of Britain, Ireland and Brittany* by Aubrey Burl. This is indispensable to the visitor, although regrettably it plays down the geomantic and astronomical side of the subject. Books on stone circles are generally conservative and huge sins of omission are common – see Further Reading for alternatives.

Safety first

Before undertaking a visit to a stone circle, the aspiring circle-spotter would do well to remember that many of the better sites lie in the mountainous regions of the British Isles. Please consider the following factors and enjoy a safe visit.

- Many hill sites involve some hard and determined walking, often up steep inclines.
- Many sites are in areas where mist and drizzle can reduce visibility suddenly, dramatically and, in some cases, dangerously.

- Most sites lie in exposed terrain where wind and driving rain prevail. It can be extremely cold in such places even in summer, with little or no shelter.
- An Ordnance Survey map and a compass are essential equipment – not least because some sites are quite hard to locate!
- Stout footware, warm and waterproof clothing and other precautions against the elements are essential when visiting sites in remote areas.
- Tell someone where you are going and your expected time of return.

If this sounds over cautious and dramatic, then it is only because the writer, along with many other regular visitors to megalithic sites, will tell you that they have endured drenching, being lost in 'instant fog', losing all feeling in fingers and toes due to cold, suffered dreadful earache due to high winds, and various other woes. Aubrey Burl sums this up by informing his readers that 'It has been a hard pleasure to see so many fine circles ...' I know just what this means!

Yet for all that, the blessing of a pilgrimage to such sites is that, on a fine day, the pleasures are immense – 60-mile visibility around the points of the compass, breath-taking scenery and gin-clear air. Sun and Moon rises and sets can touch the observer in a way which can only be felt, not explained.

CORNWALL

The Merry Maidens [SW 433 245] 19-stone circle. Easy walk. Other sites nearby.

Boscaswen-Un [SW 412 274] 19-stone ellipse. Entrance. Easy walk.

The Hurlers, Bodmin Moor [SX 259 714] Exposed site, very accessible. Three stone circles, 'male' and 'female' stones. Two large standing stones (The Pipers). Near to The Cheesewring.

DEVON

Merrivale [SX 553 746] 4 miles from Tavistock. Two stone rows, Type B circle, standing stones, cist and round houses. Sun and Moon alignments to nearby Staple Tor. Easy access from main road.

SOMERSET

Stanton Drew, Chew Magna [ST 601 631] A complex and magnificent site of many circles plus a 'cove'. Easy access but often crowded at weekends.

WILTSHIRE

Avebury [SU 103 700] The largest stone ring of all! Multiple site, with three circles, Silbury Hill, a magnificent stone avenue, longbarrows and tumuli. Easy access – popular. Large relaxing site with super neolithic museum and wholefood restaurant.

Stonehenge [SU 123 422] The most renowned circle of them all! Not an easy site to appreciate from the path. Restrictions and entry charge. Try to visit in the week, out of holiday periods. Souvenir and bookshop on site.

OXFORDSHIRE

Rollright Stones [SP 296 309] Now in charitable trust ownership, this is a lovely true circle (same diameter as the Stonehenge sarsen circle) to visit, with outlying stones. Easy access and parking.

DERBYSHIRE

Arbor Low [SK 160 636] Magnificent siting designed to be dramatic. Care with the weather here. Entrance fee, access can be boggy.

Barbrook [SK 278 755] A splendid flattened circle, with only 12 stones defining the form. Access via footpath. Two other sites within half a mile.

LANCASHIRE

Druid's Temple [SD 292 739] Concentric ring with commanding views, built with cobbled floor. Visit in winter, otherwise overgrown. Alignment to midwinter sunset.

Cumberland

Castle Rigg, Keswick [NY 291 236] A superb very early Type A flattened circle. The stones mirror the surrounding mountains and the site is built on the only flat site for miles around. Easy access – popular in summer.

Long Meg and her Daughters, Little Salkeld [NY 570 372] A superb Type B flattened circle with midwinter sunset alignment to Long Meg, which also contains a spiral carving. Easy access.

Wales

Druid's Circle, Penmaenmawr [SH 723 746] A huge ellipse, with alignments to major southern moonset. Arduous access but worth the mile walk. Other adjacent features and splendid views.

Moel ty Uchaf, Llandrillo, Bala [SJ 057 371] The best-preserved compound ring. It is possible, with care, to trace the original geometry using a rope and peg. Commanding views. Arduous access with mile walk. A nearby quartz cairn draws dowsers.

Gors Fawr, Preseli [SN 134 294] Part of the Preseli complex, which includes Parc y Meirw alignment, near Fishguard, and the bluestone site. A rather inconspicuous 16-stone ellipse, with magnificent views and a midsummer sunrise alignment at two nearby standing stones. Easy access and parking.

Scotland

Allan Water, Burgh Hill, Roxburghshire [NT 470 062] A difficult climb (25%!) to find a perfect Type I egg. Major northern moonrise alignment and splendid views.

Croft Moraig, Perthshire [NN 797 472] A fine lunar observatory, with a recumbant stone and cup and ring marks. Easy access from A7.

Druid Temple, Inverness [NH 685 420] A fine Type I egg, with possible midwinter sunset alignment. Fine views, easy access. Also the Clava complex. Too many sites to list, but Boat of Garten, Loanhead and Daviot are rewarding sites. Some concentric rings.

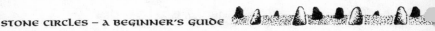

Ring of Brodgar, Orkney [HY 294 133] A splendid and huge circle henge. No charge and easy access once on Orkney.

Callanish, Outer Hebrides [NB 213 330] This important site is built rather like a Celtic cross. Fine astronomical alignments and a grandeur hard to describe. Easy access, exhibition centre nearby.

```
10 REM This is the rise and set azimuth programme for any day
       of the year
15 REM The LH column is days from spring equinox. Change day
       steps line 50
16 REM Determine the setting azimuths by reflection about
       north–south axis
20 REM The program asks for your latitude
25 REM Line 60 contains the Earth's axial tilt angle. This was
       23.95 in 2500 BCE
26 REM and may be changed (It is 23.45 today).
30 PRINT 'ENTER DESIRED LATITUDE NOW'
40 INPUT L
50 FOR T = 0 TO 365 STEP 10
60 Y = 23.95*SIN(2*3.14159*T/365.242)
70 A = COS((6.283*L)/360)
80 D = SIN((Y*6.283)/360)
90 Z = D/A
100 X = SQR((Z*Z)/(1-(Z*Z)))
110 IF T < 182 THEN Y = (ATN(X)*360/(2*3.14159) ELSE Y = 90
       + (ATN(X)*360)/2*3.14259)
120 PRINT T,Y
130 NEXT T
140 STOP
```

Program in BASIC to calculate sunrise and sunset positions throughout the year. It does not account for horizon altitude, or refraction and parallax errors.

FURThER READING

FIELD GUIDES

A Guide to the Stone Circles of Britain, Ireland and Brittany by Dr Aubrey Burl (Yale University Press, 1995). Indispensable!

EARTh MYSTERIES

Elements of Earth Mysteries by Philip Heselton (Element, 1991). A balanced guide.

DOWSING

Needles of Stone Revisited by Tom Graves (Gothic Image, 1986). Balanced guide.

The Sun and the Serpent by Hamish Miller and Paul Broadhurst (Pendragon Press, 1989). An excellent and thorough look at leylines and dowsing, beautifully presented.

Dowsing for Beginners by Naomi Ozaniek (Hodder & Stoughton, 1994).

GEOMANCY

The Ancient Science of Geomancy by Nigel Pennick (Thames & Hudson, 1979).

SACRED GEOMETRY AND MEGALITHIC SCIENCE

The Keys to the Temple by David Furlong (Piatkus, 1997).

Sun, Moon & Stonehenge by Robin Heath (Bluestone Press, 1998).

The New View over Atlantis by John Michell (Thames & Hudson, 1983)

Megalithic Sites in Britain by Alex Thom (Oxford University Press, 1967). Sadly out of print, so now only available second-hand.

MEGALITHIC ASTRONOMY

Sun, Moon & Stonehenge, as above.

Sun, Moon & Earth by Robin Heath (Wooden Books, 1999)

Sun, Moon and Standing Stones by John Edwin Wood (Oxford University Press, 1978).

Echoes of the Ancient Skies by E.C. Krupp (Oxford University Press, 1983).

Other books are mentioned in the text. Works by Keith Critchlow, Alex Thom, John Michell, John Martineau, Aubrey Burl, Rodney Castleden, Paul Devereux, Prudence Jones, Nigel Pennick, Janet and Colin Bord are all to be recommended, although there are many other good books on Paganism and earth mysteries including *Paganism*, *Earth Mysteries* and *Shamanism* by Teresa Moorey, all titles in this *Beginner's Guide* series.